WHY CANT'T BELIEVERS BELIEVE?

Reviving your heart in a troubled generation and decaying faith in God.

Written by Alphonse Okossi, PhD

WHY CANT'T BELIEVERS BELIEVE?

© 2011 Alphonse Okossi, PromiseLand Empowerment Network, Inc

All rights reserved. No part of this book may be reproduced or transmitted in any form or by any means without written permission from the author.

ISBN: 978-0-615-50057-7

ACKNOWLEDGEMENT

I would like first of all to thank God for His divine inspiration without which I would not have written this book, I would like to also thank my wife Lilleth for her encouragements and support, my children Breahna, Brittany, Esther and Joshua for their love and support without which the completion of this dissertation would not have been possible. I would like to thank Dr Mark Virkler my dissertation advisor and president of Christian Leadership University as well all who labor in the work of ministry in Christian Leadership University, Communion with God Ministries and the Koinonia Network for being a source of excellent support group and mentoring. May the Lord God Almighty bless you and keep you all.

Table of Contents

Chapter One: Introduction: Perilous times are here	2
Chapter Two: Becoming Gradually Believer In Christ	13
Chapter Three: Unbelieving Experiences in the Church	24
Chapter Four: Warnings from Biblical Prophecy	35
Chapter Three: The Cancer of Unbelief in A Christian's Life	44
Chapter Six : Identifying and Uprooting the Strongman	53
Chapter Seven: Restoring Heart Believing Faith	59
Chapter Eight: Fighting The Good Fight of Faith	67

Chapter One: Introduction: Perilous times are here

But know this, that in the last days perilous times will come: For men will be lovers of themselves, lovers of money, boasters, proud, blasphemers, disobedient to parents, unthankful, unholy, unloving, unforgiving, slanderers, without self-control, brutal, despisers of good, traitors, headstrong, haughty, lovers of pleasure rather than lovers of God, having a form of godliness but denying its power. And from such people turn away! For of this sort are those who creep into households and make captives of gullible women loaded down with sins, led away by various lusts, always learning and never able to come to the knowledge of the truth. Now as Jannes and Jambres resisted Moses, so do these also resist the truth: men of corrupt minds, disapproved concerning the faith; but they will progress no further, for their folly will be manifest to all, as theirs also was. 2 Timothy 3:1-9

One might ask why another book about faith? We already have so many on the market. I am writing this as a result of what I've experienced and learned by looking back in my own life and realizing the path I have followed to come to believe in Jesus Christ as the Son of God given to redeem me as an individual from a sure destruction.

It is easy to study God from a distance by mentally analyzing doctrines and trying to mentally make sense of them. It is easy to go to church and just play church and not show real growth, by just following a set of church protocols mixed with some Bible principles, but it is much harder to actually allow your life to be transformed by the Word of God because you actually have to put your actions into alignment with the Word and allowing it to actually change who you are. We live in a generation of people who want to be great, people who want to be in the spot light to be seen, to be famous and this has also entered the church where people want to build great religious institutions to be famous, people want to build private kingdoms and dynasties that have little to do with God's Kingdom advancement. The Hollywood lifestyle has now become the standard and goal in people's mind, so many people remain in fantasy land during their whole life time and never get to really address the matter of their heart that would set them free from the deception of this present age and world. The surest way to lose a battle is to ignore its existence while under intense fire. One important learning for me is the realization that life is a constant battle, at time invisible at time visible but in many different forms affecting any particular aspect of a person's life. Most people do not read the time in which they are in and just want to enjoy life without taking care of some deep heart issues. There is nothing wrong in enjoying life but it should not be the only goal of life, if one's goal is to enjoy life at all costs then that person may be living in denial most of his life. And trading eternal life for temporal life.

With the advance of technology it appears mankind is able to achieve great wonders, mankind can travel great distances in a very short time. With the Internet, it is now possible to access a wealth of information at the comfort one's home. From the surface it appears that all is well but when we look at the lives of people and what we all go through on a daily basis we are indeed in perilous times and in the last days. Starting from the family unit, we can see a serious devastation of the foundation of the family as designed by God. God set up the family structure to have the husband as the head of the household ruling with the wife helping in harmony and in one accord to subdue every plan, strategy and attack of the enemy against the family. Today the marriage itself is seriously under fire, there is continuous power struggle for who is really the head of the household. The children are ruling their parents instead of parent ruling them, training and teaching them the way they should go so that when they grow up they would depart from the sound godly teaching. Today even the godly teaching of the children is seriously challenged by the public school system where God is removed because of a blind interpretation of separation of church and state. Even those who want to express their Christian faith in school are often subject to sanctions and law suit. In the meantime things like Halloween and non Christian gatherings are allowed. In the media sometimes what is godly is often no longer politically correct to say in public. Preachers who truly preach the Word of God are seen as haters and sometimes sued for hate crime. Public personalities cannot publicly express their faith without being highly criticized.

When we pay a closer attention to trends in society we can see very strange things going on. Many people have tattoo on their body and they find it fun, however the majority of the tattoos refer to death, for example skull or inscription that is referring to something very strange. The fashion among the young people seems to be wearing t-shorts or shirt with picture of the dead or some inscription such as "I rather be a lion just for one day than a lamb for eternity" which really is an anti-Christ statement but those young people wearing those sometimes are church members and do not realize that it is an abomination. Christ is the Lamb of God that was slain before the foundation of the world:

saying with a loud voice: " Worthy is the Lamb who was slain To receive power and riches and wisdom, And strength and honor and glory and blessing!" Rev 5:12

Todd M. Johnson, Director, Center for the Study of Global Christianity, Gordon-Conwell Theological Seminary in a study prepared for the Pew Forum on Religion & Public Life

In 2001 states:

"Over the past 100 years, Christianity has experienced a profound southern shift in its geographical center of gravity. Whereas in 1900 over 80% of all Christians lived in Europe and Northern America, by 2005 this proportion had fallen to under 40%, and will likely fall below 30% before 2050. Table 1 shows the meteoric rise of Christianity in the South and its corresponding decline in the North."

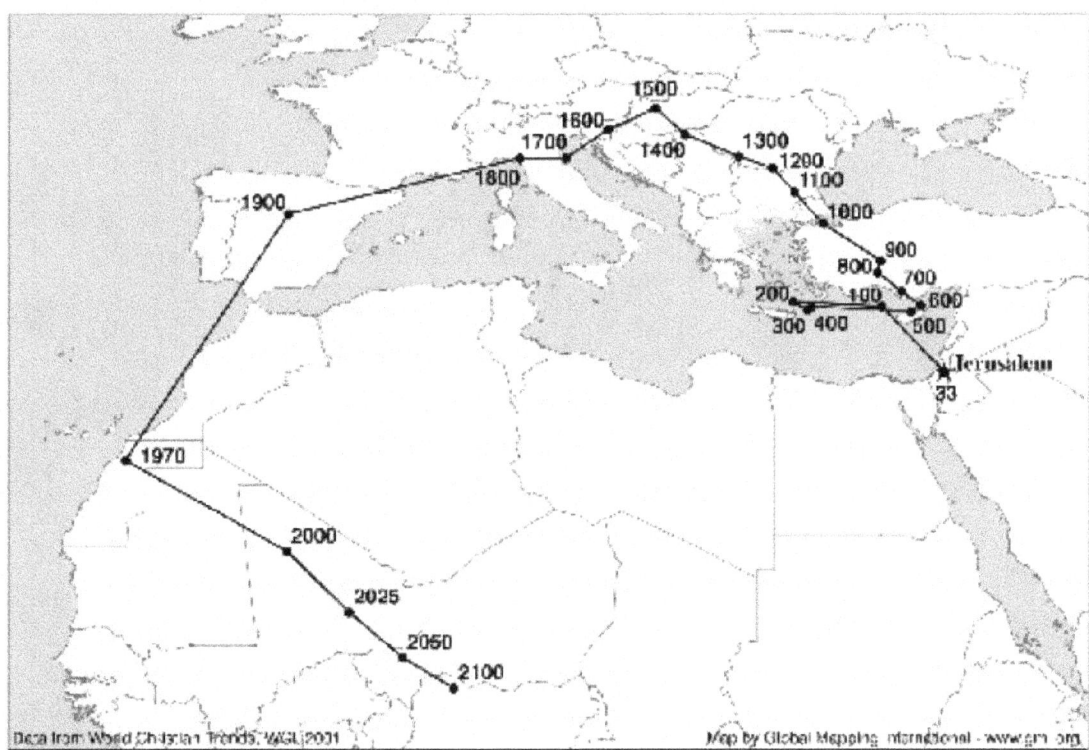

Source: Pew Forum of Religion and public life;

Actually the trend of this map is far behind because sub-Saharan Africa is currently already fast growing areas of Christianity.

It is important to look at statistical information about Christianity to see the general trend of the fight of faith.

By surveying the opinion of Christian relative to what the Word of God clearly says we can detect a measure of the fight of faith among believers:

Table 1. Survey on Views of Scripture

Views of Scripture

Biblical literalism is more common among pentecostals than among non-renewalist Christians.

% saying Scripture is actual word of God to be taken literally

	All	Pente-costals	Charis-matics	Other Christians
United States	35%	76%	48%	37%
Latin America				
Brazil	53	81	49	65
Chile	39	83	54	37
Guatemala	77	89	81	72
Africa				
Kenya	80	91	84	73
Nigeria	88	94	-	82
South Africa	59	72	72	63
Asia				
India (localities)	50	90	82	66
Philippines	53	55	49	54
South Korea	33	88	82	58

Question wording: Which one of these statements comes closest to describing your feelings about [insert "the Bible" for Christians; "the Koran" for Muslims; "Sacred Scriptures" for all others]? The [Bible is/the Koran is/ Sacred Scriptures are] the actual word of God and [is/are] to be taken literally, word for word OR [the Bible is/the Koran is/ Sacred Scriptures are] the word of God, but not everything in [it/them] should be taken literally, word for word OR [the Bible is a book/the Koran is a book/ Sacred Scriptures were] written by men and [is/are] not the word of God.

Source: Pew Forum

It is very worrisome to see that many Christians actually do not believe that the Bible is the Word of God.

Table 2. Survey on Views on Social and Moral Issues

Social and Moral Issues

Even in these very conservative countries, pentecostals often stand out for their traditional moral values.

% saying behavior is never justified

	All	Pente-costals	Charis-matics	Other Christians
United States				
Homosexuality	50%	80%	59%	54%
Drinking alcohol	29	48	42	26
Divorce	11	15	19	8
Latin America				
Brazil				
Homosexuality	49	76	46	46
Drinking alcohol	45	72	40	46
Divorce	15	37	12	15
Chile				
Homosexuality	32	64	39	30
Drinking alcohol	56	65	61	56
Divorce	21	44	31	19
Guatemala				
Homosexuality	63	73	61	61
Drinking alcohol	79	86	78	82
Divorce	47	56	46	45

% saying behavior is never justified

	All	Pente-costals	Charis-matics	Other Christians
Africa				
Kenya				
Homosexuality	98%	99%	98%	98%
Drinking alcohol	67	88	79	39
Divorce	61	70	71	51
Nigeria				
Homosexuality	98	97	-	98
Drinking alcohol	82	84	-	63
Divorce	50	81	-	79
South Africa				
Homosexuality	70	79	70	72
Drinking alcohol	52	56	52	48
Divorce	45	48	46	45
Asia				
India (localities)				
Homosexuality	72	87	86	85
Drinking alcohol	69	79	82	77
Divorce	55	74	77	60
Philippines				
Homosexuality	56	86	59	52
Drinking alcohol	57	82	57	55
Divorce	70	84	70	72
South Korea				
Homosexuality	78	90	90	86
Drinking alcohol	26	54	50	28
Divorce	37	63	53	43

Question wording: Please tell me, for each of the following statements, whether you think it can always be justified, sometimes be justified or never be justified... a. homosexuality... c. divorce... f. drinking alcohol.

Source: Pew Forum

One of the ways we can see how we are doing in our fight of faith as Christian community, is the way we react to public opinion that goes contrary to what the Word of God teaches. When the Christian community finds itself powerless facing the world values taking over society, we know that the good fight of faith is suffering losses though it will not be total.

Table 3. Survey on Divine Manifestations

Divine Healings, Divine Revelations and Exorcisms

Pentecostals are more likely than other Christians to report having experienced or witnessed divine healings, having received direct revelations from God and having experienced or seen exorcisms.

	% who have...				% who have...		
	Witnessed divine healings	Received direct revelations from God	Experienced or witnessed exorcisms		Witnessed divine healings	Received direct revelations from God	Experienced or witnessed exorcisms
				Africa			
United States - All	29%	26%	11%	Kenya - All	71%	39%	61%
Pentecostals	62	54	34	Pentecostals	87	57	86
Charismatics	46	39	22	Charismatics	78	43	67
Other Christians	28	25	7	Other Christians	47	16	39
Latin America				Nigeria - All	62	41	57
Brazil - All	38	35	34	Pentecostals	79	64	75
Pentecostals	77	64	80	Other Christians	75	46	62
Charismatics	31	28	30	South Africa - All	38	33	33
Other Christians	32	29	26	Pentecostals	73	64	60
Chile - All	26	22	13	Charismatics	47	41	40
Pentecostals	77	55	62	Other Christians	32	27	25
Charismatics	37	29	20	**Asia**			
Other Christians	24	19	8	India (localities) - All	44	17	21
Guatemala - All	56	39	38	Pentecostals	74	31	41
Pentecostals	79	59	62	Charismatics	61	18	47
Charismatics	63	39	41	Other Christians	55	23	19
Other Christians	47	39	28	Philippines - All	38	27	28
				Pentecostals	72	58	52
				Charismatics	44	35	29
				Other Christians	30	19	26
				South Korea - All	10	3	6
				Pentecostals	56	20	30
				Charismatics	61	25	35
				Other Christians	20	4	11

Question wording: Have you ever...
a. experienced or witnessed a divine healing of an illness or injury?
d. received a direct revelation from God?
e. experienced/witnessed the devil/evil spirits being driven out of a person?

Source: Pew Forum.

One interesting observation from these tables is that the Christians who experience more divine manifestations are those who are renewalist, those who tend to believe and take Scripture as face value, those who would submit to Scripture rather than manipulate it to suit their pet doctrines.

Furthermore, we note that poorer countries believers who take the Word of God as face value tend to experience more Holy Spirit manifestations such as healing, revelations, casting out demons than richer countries.

This survey of statistics points to a very important revelation about our belief system: it is better to believe the Word of God than to believe our reasoned theology, rely on acquired knowledge without the assistance of the Holy Spirit. This is actually a very old sin: the sin of knowledge of good and evil versus the tree of life. In the tree of knowledge of good and evil the carnal man is in control of his own life, therefore that person dethrones God and enthrones herself. The person who chooses the tree of life lets the Holy Spirit control her life, that person is the new spiritual man that is described in the following passage of Scripture:

I have been crucified with Christ and I no longer live, but Christ lives in me. The life I now live in the body, I live by faith in the Son of God, who loved me and gave himself for me. Galatians 2:20

This book is written to challenge Christian but also non-Christian everywhere to become more aware of a general deterioration of the moral fiber of the society and even inside the local church so that we will open our eyes and see the darkness that is covering the whole land, but that the glory of God is upon us so that we can be lights in that darkness and not be overtaken by that darkness. In Rev. 3:20, the Lord reveals a very disturbing truth about the church today

"Here I am! I stand at the door and knock. If anyone hears my voice and opens the door, I will come in and eat with him, and he with me."

How is this possible since the Lord is speaking to the churches and we know that He said in Matthew 16:18

"And I tell you that you are Peter, and on this **rock** *I will build my church, and the gates of Hades will not overcome it."*

The Lord Jesus warns us about the time we are in from the parable of the ten virgins:

"Then the kingdom of heaven shall be likened to ten virgins who took their lamps and went out to meet the bridegroom. Now five of them were wise, and five were foolish. Those who were foolish took their lamps and took no oil with them, 4 but the wise took oil in their vessels with their lamps. 5 But while the bridegroom was delayed, they all slumbered and slept.

"And at midnight a cry was heard: 'Behold, the bridegroom is coming;[a] go out to meet him!' Then all those virgins arose and trimmed their lamps. And the foolish said to the wise, 'Give us some of your oil, for our lamps are going out.' But the wise answered, saying, 'No, lest there should not be enough for us and you; but go rather to those who sell, and buy for yourselves.' And while they went to buy, the bridegroom came, and those who were ready went in with him to the wedding; and the door was shut.

"Afterward the other virgins came also, saying, 'Lord, Lord, open to us!' But he answered and said, 'Assuredly, I say to you, I do not know you.' "Watch therefore, for you know neither the day nor the hour[b] in which the Son of Man is coming. **Matthews 25:1-13**

These signs that we see today should compel us to watch and pray and keep the faith, we should know that God exist put our complete faith in Him and diligently seek Him all the days of our lives. In this parable, the lamp is like the Word of God and the oil is like the Holy Spirit. Every Christian needs to put his faith and walk by faith in the Word of God and the Spirit of God to lead us into all truth. We are truly living in the night because we live in a fallen world that is under the dominion of the evil one. We need our lamp and a lot of oil to be able to make it through the night. We need to be full of the Holy Spirit to be able to make it through this dark world.

We live indeed in perilous times, every single moment of a believer who truly believes is under attack from the one who comes only to kill to steal and to destroy. Let's not be ignorant of his devices. No one living on this earth is totally free from his direct or indirect influence; the saying "new level, new devils" is true. One may think because someone has been serving the Lord for fifty years, surely the enemy cannot tempt him, yes he can because he was trying the same with Jesus, he even used Peter's mouth to speak and Jesus rebuked him for that (*Peter took him aside and began to rebuke him. "Never, Lord!" he said. "This shall never happen to you!" Jesus turned and said to Peter, "Get behind me, Satan! You are a stumbling block to me; you do not have in mind the concerns of God, but merely human concerns."* Matthew 16:22-23). We need to understand that the enemy's attacks are specific to our weakness so what he uses on another person may not be the same thing he uses on you. That's why when we put our faith in God and move by faith the devil will not be able to use any weakness of ours but will be forced to reveal his nature. The enemy can influence a believer to even use Scripture in a wrong way:

Carefully identify how the enemy influenced Aaron in the wilderness in the following passage:

When the people saw that Moses was so long in coming down from the mountain, they gathered around Aaron and said, "Come, make us gods[a] who will go before us. As for this fellow Moses who brought us up out of Egypt, we don't know what has happened to him." Aaron answered them, "Take off the gold earrings that your wives, your sons and your daughters are wearing, and bring them to me." So all the people took off their earrings and brought them to Aaron. He took what they handed him and made it into an idol cast in the shape of a calf, fashioning it with a tool. Then they said, "These are your gods,[b] Israel, who brought you up out of Egypt." When Aaron saw this, he built an altar in front of the calf and announced, "Tomorrow there will be a festival to the LORD." So the next day the people rose early and sacrificed burnt offerings and presented fellowship offerings. Afterward they sat down to eat and drink and got up to indulge in revelry. Exodus 32:1-6

The enemy used the fact that Aaron was intimidated by the people and because he was not the one who was hearing from God. This shows how Aaron was disconnected from God compared to Moses who did nothing without consulting the Lord. Today there are many Aaron's in the body of Christ who stop believing who called them and started doing their own things. They start having programs in the church that have no influence on the spiritual growth of the people.

Sometimes they even become obstacles to the growth of their own flock. These believers moving in their own wisdom, trying to help God in their own strength sometimes can be influenced by the enemy to:
- use Scripture to justify evil just like the Pharisees
- use Scripture to tear down others instead of building them up by having judgmental attitudes instead of allowing themselves to receive revelation from God and have mercy on others
- using Scripture to divide instead of unite such as futile denominational fights
- modernize Scripture understanding to justify pagan belief

A Rising Oppressive World Power System

With the advent of the Internet the whole world has become like a big village because anyone in the world can communicate live anytime and for free via instant messaging, text ,messaging, video conversation, documents sharing etc... Anyone can upload a video or any other web content that can be viewed by anyone in the world.

Furthermore the world international organizations such as UN with its satellite organizations originally created to prevent worldwide wars, foster humanitarian aids and keep world peace have now become a cleverly orchestrated world system to oppress the smaller countries. That is because world economic and political super-powers have the effective power within these international organizations to influence small countries political and economic trend and development. This is clearly obvious in the relationship between France and the old French colonies, where French documentaries have shown that the French government exercise extreme power over elections, selection of key leaders of those old colonies. The most vibrant example is the gross interference of the UN and France in a regular election in the ivory Coast in 2010 that end up in a complete state of confusion. In some situations mysterious assassinations of head of states, prominent presidential candidates who fight for true independence were conducted by the French government to maintain their colonies in new state of bondage. The super-powers use their effective control and monopoly of the news to practically shape the world news and world opinion of an issue. So what they say becomes the "truth" no matter what the real "Truth" is. The small countries have no way to defend themselves against such system except they make God their Lord.

I see this world system as a laboratory of the anti-Christ government where the future anti-Christ person will use those techniques learned from this world system after having perfected them, to rule the world. That rule will be founded on lies, oppression, manipulations, intimidations and control tactics particularly of the major news media agencies and companies, perfected over the ages, as well as on the advance of technology that would create fake miracles and wonders to deceive those who have stopped to believe in Christ and live by faith in Him.

All what is happening in the families, communities and world system clearly point to the fact that there is a spiritual war raging at all levels to control the people and the regions of the world. As believers we know because the Bible warns us, we must therefore believe in what God has given us through His prophetic words written for us in the Bible.

The present world system is like a big human being looking really good from the outside but internally it is full of decaying diseased cells because they no longer can hold together and therefore seems to be slowly going to a certain death. This is really a description of Cancer. Cancer can attack any organ of the body and its purpose is to destruction at the cellular level until the whole organism finally dies. Wonder why there is such a widespread of that disease in the natural sense. In the spiritual the real cancer is unbelief and lack of faith in God. Since *"God resists the proud, But gives grace to the humble"* (in James 4:6) the more we move in unbelief the farther away we move from God, the source of Life. Unbelief has babies and they are selfishness and lack of love, love that is needed to keep the whole organism together:

From him the whole body, joined and held together by every supporting ligament, grows and builds itself up in love, as each part does its work.
Ephesians 4:15.

When we are a believer but do not believe we can justify any sin with some out of context and fleshly interpretation of Scripture. This book is written to wake up and prepare the believer in Christ for the end of time or to avoid destruction before the end of times.

Any time there is excessive sin where good is seen as bad and bad seen as good, destruction is at the door because that is what happened in Sodom and Gomorrah. When those who believe in God are rare destruction is near. O that the believers in Jesus would wake up and see that this generation is following the ways of Sodom and the fashions of Gomorrah and that this is the time to wake up from whatever spiritual sleep we are in, and be serious about our faith just like Abraham stayed before God and pleaded for the righteous of the land and be a voice crying in the wilderness, like Noah preaching that it will rain and that the flood will come while people were going on their daily routine until the flood came and took them away..

Chapter Two: Becoming Gradually Believer In Christ

But seek ye first the kingdom of God, and his righteousness; and all these things shall be added unto you. Math. 6:33

I was born in a small village of West Africa from two poor and unschooled parents, my father passed away when I was still a baby. In my village, witchcraft, sorcery and idolatry were common everyday life activities of the majority of the community. Thank God there were also one Catholic Church, one Protestant Methodist church and one Assembly of God church that presented the Gospel of Jesus Christ in different way in this occult practice dominated environment. My mother took us to the Catholic Church every major holiday. Looking back now, I thank God that they did.

At a very young age, about 10, I was frequently hearing travelling evangelist ministers of the Gospel preaching on the street about the end of the world and how people who do evil will go to hell. This preaching created such a fear in my heart and stuck with me until now and it was one of the things that caused me to become a Christian believer. I believe my heart was truly drawn to Christ from that time since that fear help me distance myself from the ungodly practices all around me and kept me from bowing to the Baal of the land.

I was taught in the western education system from my primary to my college education I was taught in a French education system that gives little place for God and the accumulation of knowledge as the only valid way for knowing. After that I was trained in the US for my graduate education under the same conditions.

I was trained to use my brain power as the main source of knowing, despising anything that cannot be proven scientifically such as knowing from vision, dreams and any other spiritual gifts founded on the Word of God, though I had many visions and dream at my young age. I trusted my acquired knowledge and status more than God.

My western education background had a powerfully negative effect on me concerning my faith in God. Ironically, my background as a person who has witnessed in several occasions the display of occultist power by others in the community with visible manifestations throughout my whole life helped me out. It helped me reject the negative impact of the western education concerning my faith in God. I knew that God exists, strangely this is something that very common in the traditional African culture, and that the spiritual world - good or bad - exists and so no theoretical or philosophical discourse could prove to me or convict me otherwise because of what I have already experienced. Furthermore I believe the Lord was protecting me from losing the fear of God I got from listening to messages of heaven and hell. The hold of the Lord was so strong that when I start believing in the power of the devil the truth of the Gospel helped me regain godly perspective; whenever I did something that is sinful I felt strong sorrow.

I can see now looking back how the Lord was truly and continues to be the Author and Finisher of my faith. The little faith I received when I heard the

Christian evangelist preach about heaven and hell and how we have the choice to follow Jesus and go to heaven, truly helped me to bounce back every time.

Because of the devastation of witchcraft activities that most people in Africa experience on a regular basis, most western educated people seek to 'protect' themselves from witchcraft attacks by either entering a local or international occultist society or believing in Jesus Christ and being serious about their faith in Him. There was no middle ground because of the fear that the witches would simply eliminate them.

Witnessing a mixture of Christianity and occultism along with the message of the evangelist I heard talking about hell and end of the world created some confusion in me for a time. I felt without purpose for a long time, a time of questioning on everything I knew. I learn and consider to be my goal in life to get excellent education, get a well paying job, climb the ladder of society, get married and have children, going to church occasionally and limiting my Christianity to just going to church and may be giving some money and time to the church as long as they don't interfere with my set goal in life. I considered my life pillars to be my education and my career.

A Time of Disillusion

For a time my goal in life was working pretty well, I got married with my wife Lilleth the week after I graduated with my PhD in Economics. I immediately got a big job in a multi-country government monetary union institution where I was pretty successful. Then I moved back to the US, got another job and was living quite well until a long series of job losses and unstable income stream brought me to a point where all my life pillars were literally taken away one after the other. This was a serious time of testing and pruning that took about four years of instable income flow eben though I was able to always get contract jobs during the period, thank God for His provision.

Personal Encounter with the Holy Spirit, Experiencing God as Omni-present and Omniscient

Before the period of trials I was baptized and was faithfully attending a Church of God of Prophecy church in Albany New York area and one day I clearly received the Holy Spirit in a special way in a church service. This encounter that was very real to me helped me to be more committed to God. This also helped me realize that God is not far but near, right inside.

Knowing God to be the Provider

Just before the period of trial started my wife and I just bought a house and I was the one making most of the money for the family, at the time also we were expecting our son Joshua and we already have three girls, Breahna, Brittany and Esther. The situation was very fearful to me because I had never thought that this could happen to me but it did.

One thing that I learned for sure was that we never missed any meal, we still have our two cars and we were always able to make our mortgage payments every month.

Knowing God as the Teacher and that God Speaks to us if we are willing to listen

During the time of hardship, I spent more time in reading my Bible and thinking about what I read seeking to understand what God meant, and praying and journaling the impressions I was receiving. It was a time I experienced many visions, dreams and revelation from Scripture and even some specific things I needed to do. I also received from many independent ministers as well as through my personal seeking the Lord to verify those claims, the call to ministry of the Gospel, something that did not even register on my 'radar screen' in my life prior to going into the time of hardship.

In Retrospect, I Known God as the Redeemer of my life

Looking back to my whole life from infancy I can say that without the Lord's hands on me, I had very little if any chance at all of getting to where I am. The Lord has delivered me from sicknesses because of the harsh condition in which I was born and raised up, diseases, witchcraft and occultism. I have seen many young people who have been victims of those and did not make it. I am realizing more and more that there were many temptations and baits and distractions in my life that the Lord has delivered me from.

Increased awareness that God is leading me to carry out a specific purpose for Him

I was not consistently going to church before but I became a truly more committed in 1993 after I graduated from State University at Albany with a PhD in economics and got married. This time marked a turning point because it was time to settle and start being serious about my relationship with God. From that time I was faithfully attending Sunday school and receiving formal teaching on the whole Bible and also church conventions, retreats and various meetings that helped build my Biblical foundation. In 1996 I received the baptism of the Holy Spirit and was given responsibilities (member of financial committee, among the leadership of the men's ministry, member of men's choir) in the church (Church of God of Prophecy). These positions helped me understand how the local church functions and many issues church leaders have to face in leading a flock, then later in 1999, I was ordained deacon and assisted the pastor of the local Church of God of Prophecy, pastor Pagel J. Williams in the leadership of the local church. Later I was also ordained Minister of the Gospel and Christian counseling.

I believe the Lord has blessed my life to get my education debt free from High School to graduate school, coming from a challenging life in a rural area of Ivory Coast (West Africa). The Lord has literally delivered me from a dangerous environment that could have had the best of me physically, emotionally as well as spiritually.

Experiencing God continually and gradually in many different ways

I am now more open to experience God in every area of life not just in a local church worship setting. One example of this is that one day I was driving on the I-55 highway from Romeoville to Chicago when I saw a truck carrying many heavy tools driving at high speed, as it passed me I noticed a large hatchet inside and my eyes were fixed on that particular tool without any particular thought for a few minutes then all of the sudden it flew out of the truck and stated bouncing wildly all over the highway. But because my eyes have already identified it I was able to quickly navigate away from it. I thanked the Lord for watching over me because this could have been fatal for me.

I particularly realized that once I was serious about obeying the Word of God in my life I experienced persecution from very unlikely places. The walk of faith cannot take place without a fight. It seems as though there is an invisible frontier that the person walking by faith must cross and on that border there are border patrols of all types: some of those people we trust, some are authority figure we submit to, some have family or marriage link with the faith walker, some have power to stop us. One thing that stands out is that all those people sometimes without really knowing what they are doing or thinking they are trying to help you avoid destruction are actually playing right in the hand of the enemy to stop what God has put before us to achieve.

I discovered that we cannot second guess the vision God has given us. We must first make sure that it is coming from God then we must be submitted to the Holy Spirit to lead us and walk by faith and not by doubt.

Gradual understanding that everyone is involved in a personal spiritual war

Anyone who really wants to know can realize that every single decision that we make will be faced with some opposition, every hat we wear in life has its own life challenges to overcome. It is as if every individual living his live is drawing a nice picture on a blank board but as the person starts to draw there is another mean guy with an eraser in his hand wiping off that nice picture, making the work of the drawing frustrating and counterproductive. I also gradually understood that even though that person who is being counterproductive to the drawer's work may be a person we actually know and may even be close to us, he or she is not the enemy, he or she is a victim or hostage of the real enemy who is the devil. We do not fight against flesh and blood but against principalities, powers, and spiritual wickedness in high places. Then I have the understanding that sometimes the best way to see what is going on in the spiritual realm in our lives is to carefully observe what is going on naturally that seems to be an invisible barrier that we are not able to cross no matter our skills, financial blessing, natural or spiritual gifts. This has no distinction for whether one is a lay-minister, a full time minister, a well known five-fold minister, a congregation member or a non believer. This type of fight is general, because if Jesus has to rebuke Peter in the following passage, there is no one who cannot be touched by the enemy: *But He turned and said to Peter, "Get behind Me, Satan! You are an offense to Me, for you are not mindful of the things of God, but the things of men." Matthew 16:23.*

It is as if there was a register where every single family of the earth throughout all generation is carefully recorded. This is done for the recorder to identify if there were some type of treaty or alliance in one of our ancestors who lived a life of sin. If there were any and chances are there were, then the enemy can use that as a door to access an area of our life to start his destructive work. The enemy can use whatever our forefather did to gain access to our lives today and claim things. When we decide to escape that bondage by becoming Christians we face special opposition because we are basically braking free from the bondage of satan or secular alliances he formed with our forefathers. Thank be to God that brings us from the kingdom of darkness into His Kingdom of Light through the finished work of the Lord Jesus Christ.

It is true that we are in a spiritual war that has a wide array of natural manifestations and the natural mind is blind to it so that it can remain bound to the devil. We also know that the devil robbed the authority God has given to mankind through the sin of Adam that made this possible. Thank God that we have regained our place in God when we come to Jesus. Since we live in a battle ground we cannot ignore the war that is going on. If we do, we will become victim of that war. That war that we have to fight is by faith in Jesus Christ and what He has done. The only way we can win that war is if we live by faith in Jesus. Because

Jesus has already done the complete requirement for our redemption we have continual victory if we remain in faith in God through Jesus. The spiritual fight we are talking about is not a fight for our salvation – that has been acquired by us believing in our heart and with our mouth confessing Christ as our Lord and Savior – this fight is a fight to maintain ourselves in our promise land. Just as Joshua and the Israelites have to move by faith to be victorious in the promise land, we have to also move and walk and fight by faith in Jesus Christ for our individual lives trying to reach our life goals (or promise lands). Of course salvation has to take us through the wilderness (which are the challenges we face while we are moving toward our life goals by faith in God) from the deliverance from our own 'Egypt' (i.e. when and/or where we were still in darkness) to our promise land when we are maturing in faith. Even when we mature in faith we still have giants to fight in the land (our land can be the sphere of authority, territory or gifts God entrusted to us) God has given to us. The sad thing about this is that many die in their own wilderness because of unbelief or fail to keep their faith in God. They allow those brothers or sisters who do not believe to contaminate their faith just as the ten spies out of the twelve who went to spy on the promise land and brought a negative report. They convicted a whole generation with this bad report and because of that; God let them perish in the wilderness never putting their foot in the promise land.

This understanding makes one to be more compassionate and patient with people because we love them and want them to be free from whatever is holding them hostage in an area of life.

We can make mistakes as we seek to move in faith

Some of the mistakes I made were to grow impatient as the Lord was showing me His vision of my life or what I understood from the vision at that time. As I grew impatient I felt trapped and wanted something better.

The common mistake is to take what a Christian brother or sister or leader is doing to us or saying to us, personal. Since we are not fighting against flesh and blood we know that there is always some evil spirit behind them trying to deceive and bring division. One common reaction following a rejection is to fire back and start slandering that person, but this too is a bait of the enemy to cause us to sin so that he can have access to attack us.

Furthermore if we hold resentment or bitterness against our brother we not only open up the accusative door to the enemy to attack him but also a door to attack our health and intimacy with God. We should not be ignorant of the devices of the enemy.

We are not talking about studying the enemy or giving him too much importance, we are talking about knowing his tricks and turn the light on him so that he can run from us. We know that we cannot defeat the enemy on our own strength but we can always defeat him by faith in Christ. The following is another story showing some of the way the enemy tries to trap a whole community through ungodly traditional practices:

It is in the tradition of many tribes in Africa to do many seemingly harmless traditional ceremonies when a person dies. This includes requesting liquor from the family of the deceased and "speaking to the dead ancestors", poring some of the liquor on the floor for that purpose. Sometimes animals are killed to honor the dead and ancestors. Since people have been doing those practices for centuries, the current generation including saved Christians, just does it without any questioning about the meaning of those practices. However these practices by their nature are unbiblical and honor the deads because when the now deceased person was alive the kind of money spent to bury him is way more than he had ever received in his or her life.

I came to face these traditional practices when I lost my uncle. While the elders of the village were requesting all kinds of traditional things to carry on their practices, the Lord was dealing with me that I should not take part of that. When I started to confront some of the elders privately to explain what those practices really mean, they could not explain. By that time they have already received what they requested from the hand of my elder brother who is the head of the family. I started to refuse every other thinks that they required from me personally. Later on we prayed for my brother for protection. Because they had already done their practices before I started to react, I had to pay for some of the consequences and had to repent from what was done.

I encourage therefore that anyone who finds himself in this type of situation should stand firmly on his faith in God and not allow any village elder use tradition to bully them into serious bondage. It really is a serious bondage because it is as if they were making a covenant with the deads using their money and the gifts the village elders required of them, tying them as well as their finances to the spirit of death.

Thank be to God who had mercy on me and delivered me and continue to deliver me from all my fears and gave me His perspective, though I have to continue to deal with the effect of some of the mistakes I made at that time.

Thank also be to God that He has provided grace through faith in Him, so that we can repent from dead works and reconcile with God.

Unfinished journey

My new perspective of life is that life is what we make of it and so I should maximize every moment and not allow discouragement, laziness and all kinds of mind binding things in life, reduce my momentum to mature in my faith in God. I know challenges will be in my path so I pray that the Lord give me strength and determination to pursue and overcome all of them because He calls us to be overcomers. Since we are overcomers we should act like overcomers, walk like overcomers even when we are facing adversity.

Life Experience of the Word of God, the best teacher

One important life lesson I learned is that the experiences of life that bring us to the Word of God are excellent teachers. An experience is marked on our heart like inscriptions burnt in a stone tablet. This is something many of the best years of education cannot easily achieve.

Marital challenges

One area of my Christian faith where I have been most challenged is the marital relationship. The Scripture is pretty clear what the will of God is in the marriage relationship. However the culture around us seem to advocate another way that seem more "loving" in the world standard. Worst sometimes even preachers try to appease the wives or the husbands when talking about God will in the marriage not to offend any instead of using the Word to correct, instruct and edify the marriages. What that does it to allow anything to take place and continue the confusion in the marriage relationship and the family.

Financial hardship due to job losses

After a few job losses and financial hardship, my faith was really challenged because I was trusting and continues to trust that God is my Provider; the challenge is when one is inside the "fire" it looks as though I will never get out of it, particularly because the situation of unemployment attracts so many marital arguments and is a time a severe humiliation for the man not being able to provide. The interesting and really liberating fact is that God has provided during all this time of hardship, no meals were missed; we had a roof over our heads.

Losing hope on children because of behavior and performance in a society where correcting your child may send you to jail

The Bible teaches us to correct our children and not spear the rod of correction; however the legal system sometimes sets boundaries that were supposed to protect children from abuse which is a good thing; however the same laws restrict a godly parent from biblically correcting the disobedient children. The bottom line is that we don't want the government to raise our children since that is what would happen if the parent is sent to jail and the government takes charge of the children. So sometimes the environment in which one lives can be toxic for one's faith work.

Losing trust on Christian leaders because of some fleshly action and misplaced words

One the most damaging thing in a believer's life is experiencing rejection from a Christian leader one loves and trusts. It is even more damaging if that leader appears to consistently avoids and ignores you. But the fact is that we live in a fallen world where the enemy finds a ways to infiltrate even the highest level of the people of God to create divisions and distract the purpose of God on the believers of a congregation.

Struggling with some passage of Scripture that totally go against reason

Eating Jesus Flesh and Drinking Jesus Blood

Verily, verily, I say unto you, He that believeth on me hath everlasting life. I am that bread of life. Your fathers did eat manna in the wilderness, and are dead. This is the bread which cometh down from heaven, that a man may eat thereof, and not die. I am the living bread which came down from heaven: if any man eat of this bread, he shall live for ever: and the bread that I will give is my flesh, which I will give for the life of the world.

The Jews therefore strove among themselves, saying, How can this man give us his flesh to eat? Then Jesus said unto them, Verily, verily, I say unto you, Except ye eat the flesh of the Son of man, and drink his blood, ye have no life in you. Whoso eateth my flesh, and drinketh my blood, hath eternal life; and I will raise him up at the last day. For my flesh is meat indeed, and my blood is drink indeed. He that eateth my flesh, and drinketh my blood, dwelleth in me, and I in him. As the living Father hath sent me, and I live by the Father: so he that eateth me, even he shall live by me. This is that bread which came down from heaven: not as your fathers did eat manna, and are dead: he that eateth of this bread shall live for ever. These things said he in the synagogue, as he taught in Capernaum. Many therefore of his disciples, when they had heard this, said, This is an hard saying; who can hear it? When Jesus knew in himself that his disciples murmured at it, he said unto them, Doth this offend you? John 6:47-61 (King James Version)

This is one conversation that Jesus had with the religious leaders as well as the Pharisees listening to Him that day. Jesus was very explicit and even graphic, insisting that one must eat his flesh and drink his blood to have life, that his flesh was food indeed. Even some of Jesus' disciples were so grossed out that they left him that day. But I believe the Lord was challenging the faith of the people, by challenging their reason. If they really believe then they would not rely on reason but on their faith to have the true understanding of what Jesus was teaching them, because what Jesus was saying was spiritual and only the spiritual man in God's image would truly understand.

Many times in our own life we face situations such as this where our reason challenges our faith. We face situation when the mind is telling us that moving in faith is foolish and if we keep pondering in our mind we will convince ourselves to move by reason rather than by faith: Hebrews 11:6 says *But without faith it is impossible to please Him, for he who comes to God must believe that He is, and that He is a rewarder of those who diligently seek Him.* So in reality it is better to be foolish and believe in and move on what God said than following our flawed reasoning which is based on flawed understanding. Dr Mark Virkler, the President of Christian Leadership University said in many of his teachings that *"when reason challenges faith, reason is always wrong"*, I truly believe this statement because Romans 8:7 validates it *Because the carnal mind is enmity against God; for it is not subject to the law of God, nor indeed can be.*

In many situations, the enemy will use someone who trusts in his or her carnal thinking to discourage the person who wants to take God Word as face value and obey it.

O beloved brothers and sisters, I plead that we wake up from our spiritual sleep and take a look at the time we are in, a time making Sodom and Gomorrah look like a joke! There is a time to repent and fully engage in the fight, the real fight worth fighting - the good fight of faith - because if at time God brought punishment upon His own people Israel what make us think that He will continue to tolerate a generation of worst than Sodomites and making the sin of the people of Gomorrah look like a joke. We should remember that grace does not work if we deliberately and boldly choose unbelief and rebellion over belief and faith in God. Let's remember that some of Israel was broken of the tree because of unbelief. Let's therefore believe what God says and not try to interpret it.

Chapter Three: Unbelieving Experiences in the Church

You search the Scriptures, for in them you think you have eternal life; and these are they which testify of Me. John 5:39

There is nothing more hurtful than declaring with zeal our Christianity and yet behaving just as the worst of the unbelievers. In the Bible the Pharisees were an excellent representation of this phenomenon. The Pharisees were the top religious leaders who were the ones who knew the Scriptures and taught them to the rest of Israel who depended on them to know the will of God. Yet when the Word-Became-Flesh came among them they rejected Him, harassed His ministry, accused Him of operating under the influence of demons and finally killed Him. Thank God he cannot be killed because He is Life. The truth is that it is not the knowledge of the Bible that will give eternal life automatically but the living faith in the Lord Jesus Christ:

You search the Scriptures, for in them you think you have eternal life; and these are they which testify of Me. John 5:39

We know that the devil is not inheriting eternal life but eternal death, yet the devil knows the Scriptures. We need the Spirit of God to help us understand the Word of God and change our heart:

who also made us sufficient as ministers of the new covenant, not of the letter but of the Spirit;[a] for the letter kills, but the Spirit gives life. 2 Corinthians 3:6

Every believer in Christ must really believe what the Bible says. That is easier said than done because it is a battle, a continual spiritual battle that manifests itself in practically every area of the believer's life. The Bible instructs to fight the good fight of faith.

Why do we have to fight for our faith, for what we believe? I believe that this is the fundamental question that every believer must answer for him or herself. The answer lies in the fact that Satan still has the power to deceive and this is enough to bring people into captivity taking the form of apathy, apostasy, hypocrisy etc...

The purpose of this survey is to show some of the outward evidences of the inner war of faith, to look at the life of others around us throughout our lives up to this point as well as from listening to people who experienced some issues, and identify their faith experience and the uniqueness of their spiritual battle and journey. This will help us better keep God's perspective in every area of our lives.

The following stories have been altered to protect the privacy of the people involved but to expose the sin. This is so that the readers can recognize it and set him or herself free if he/she finds him or herself entangled in those situations by putting their faith in the Lord rather than in a man or woman. Some are purely stories to describe something that is going on in the Body of Christ that I became aware of.

An interesting conversation of a famous pastor, Nemo with his staff

Pastor Nemo is a very successful pastor, in the world's standard of success that is. Successful in the sense that his church that he built after departing abruptly from the church where he was serving, is run very well, membership is large, they have a TV ministry and are involved in many visible activities, however the membership growth is sluggish. A family member, a close relative or a close friend held all the most senior position of the church. Everything seems perfect from the outside. Here is a fictitious story based on personal experience and others about pastor Nemo way of doing business, likely to describe one of the high level senior staff meeting:

"How many people joined the church this month? Asked pastor Nemo?

"Forty replied one of his ministers"

"What is their total combined family income from the survey form?"

$2,400,000 replied the membership management director. 12 families make up about half of that and the rest of the families, the remaining amount.

"I supposed you taught them about our tithe and offering commandments, we have to get them to pay their tithes and offerings" replied pastor Nemo. Also make sure the family with high income gets the usual preferential treatment.

"12 of them expressed that they believe God has called them into ministry and their interest of coming was to learn so that they can pursue their call wherever it might be" sarcastically reported the membership management director.

"You know we do not have time for dreamers, but let them fully join and we will get the dreams out of their mind, there is only one vision here. They come here to serve wherever I put them and they need to learn good character. Once they join, make sure you use the usual intimidation tactics; I want to know everything they are doing. Also arrange a secret meeting between myself and each spouse of the dreamers. We need to discourage them. You come in my territory I decide your life, we open the door, when they join, we close the door, no one is allowed to get out in his own willing without my approval. I am going to preach against those church hoppers and how they are bad for the church as usual."

"But Pastor why not just meet them directly and hear from them if they are genuinely called by God and disciple them appropriately" asked the evangelistic outreach director.

"Son" angrily replied the Pastor Nemo, "I have been in ministry for thirty five years and I know this type of people, beside you cannot keep this church in the family if you just allow anyone to come and start attracting people to them because of their spiritual gifts."

The evangelist director go further to share "John says in his epistle, *the anointing which ye have received of him abideth in you, and ye need not that any man teach you*" (1John2:27) and 1Timothy 2:5 says *"there is one mediator between God and Men, the man Christ Jesus"* and Psalms 118:8 says *"it is better to trust in the Lord than to put confidence in Man"* and 1 John 4:4 says *"You, dear children, are from God and have overcome them, because the one who is in you is greater than the one who is in the world."* So should we not stop judging them and let God judge them and give them the benefit of the doubt?

Burning with anger, Pastor Nemo expelled the evangelist director from the meeting and fired him on the spot. So fear gripped all the other members of the meeting and no one dared to say anything against Pastor Nemo's teachings, ways and leadership style. During the following six months Pastor Nemo teachings and preaching were solely directed to people who he believes are not loyal to him or want to leave his church, he often voices that he would write about the "non-loyal" members in his books by name and that wherever they go he will personally make sure that they would not succeed. He even invited trusted other pastors to come to preach about the topic just to discourage the dreamers. Worse of all the congregation put on themselves to go after anyone who attempts to leave the church using some mind game and isolation, manipulations and intimidations. Families who have people who could discern that spirit of manipulation, intimidation and control experience serious family problems even divorce in some. One of Pastor Memo's favorite teaching is to encourage spouse to leave the other spouse who want to leave the church because of the doctrine taught and strongly command that spouse to leave the other spouse who wants to leave.

This fictitious story is based on how the world sees most pastors and the church. The main goal was to expose the sin that plagues the leadership in that type of church.

How does this story relate to the work of faith?

First, the faith of pastor Nemo is tested to see if his ministry leadership style is consistent with what Jesus taught and lived or is it a method of the world or of the Pharisees (see Matthew 23:2-13). Hypocrisy characterizes the leadership style of the Pharisees. Secondly the faith work of each person working for pastor Nemo is tested because they have to struggle between what they understand from Scripture themselves and the teaching and dealing of pastor Nemo that are unscriptural. When they realize that something unscriptural is going on, they know that Scripture teaches them to confront the person as an member of the eldership team, however because pastor Nemo's teaching involve a systematic discouragement of anyone challenging him in any issue by manipulation, intimidation and control techniques, those enlightened elders in the team are caught in some type of captivity that they struggle with daily, just as Nicodem a Pharisee who came secretly to see Jesus (John 3:1-3), did. However the answer is not very hard since Scripture teaches us to obey our elders in the Lord but that Jesus Christ alone is Lord over all. They must choose obedience to God rather than sacrifice and loyalty to man. They must confront in a Biblical way and if they get fired so be it at least they have obeyed God.

Frustration of an Enlightened Brother in Christ

Brother Ray has been going to his parent's church since he was little. His parents are devout Christians of a major Christian denomination. His father is a deacon and his mother is a minister in the church. The church denomination is very strict about manifestation of any spirit, they demonize and cast out of the church anyone who claims to have heard from God or experienced divine revelation through dream and vision.

What this does to the faith walker is to attack their faith by sowing confusion in the mind of the one who is truly seeking to know and obey the Truth.

How would anyone's faith resist such stronghold of spiritual wickedness in high place? Thank God that our Lord is in control and is the only Author and Finisher of our faith.

Conversation with a Sister Fed up with Church because of a few hypocrite church folks

Sister Natalie a regular member of the church has been practicing spiritual discipline of continual prayer, meditation of the Scripture and what the pastor preaches, and periodic fasting to seek God and hear from God for over fifteen years. She now gets insights and revelation from God on a regular basis. However her pastor who has been pasturing the local church for over three decade is hooked up on so many programs that he does not have any time for God, his prayers are short and lacking in power. For this reason many in the church go to her to be ministered rather that to the pastor. The pastor became enraged against Sister Natalie and refused to promote her or give her any ministering task. Furthermore the pastor often uses the pulpit on Sunday morning preaching to openly chastise Natalie for being rebellious because she is accepting to minister to the people even though she inform the pastor of her prayer ministry activity with any member or outside believer. Natalie has been frustrated for this behavior that she thinks is unfair to her and starts to walk away from the church. Natalie thought "I bet if I remain a baby Christian all my life he would be happier because what the Lord is doing through my life will not have to challenge him. Are we not to work out our own soul salvation by allowing the Holy Spirit to counsel us concerning everything? "

There is nothing more damaging to the trust and the faith of a person than to see the person that he trusts most and dearly love, starts to accuse him and mistreat him. The faith walk of Natalie is severely shaken because of the reaction of her pastor that she truly respects as a man of God.

An interesting conversation with a lady on the train, sharing the Gospel of Christ to her:

The lady seemed frustrated and stressed out on the train, I felt that the Lord wanted me to say some encouragement to her, as we got out of the train and were walking toward to streets of Chicago loop around Union Station; as I was walking I noticed that someone's hand hit mine and I saw that it was the same lady I saw on the train. Then I asked her how she was doing? She said good thank you. Then I said that she was a good person and that God loved her. I saw her countenance changed and she seemed very pleased. Then I said do you go to church? And she responded, sometimes. I said great. Then for some reason I was led to tell her that when she goes to church she is going there for God, and that she should not focus on what people are doing. Then she thanked me and said that what I said was very profound to her and made her day. She went further to say that she was very discouraged lately with people in her church and has stopped attending because she felt that people were constantly judging her and she felt like the church treated her worst than the people of the world. I said I am sorry about that but she should only focus on her Lord Jesus and not let haters destroy her relationship with her Lord and Savior. She thanked me and we went in different directions.

Younger faith walkers tend to identify who God is by observing the leadership of the church and the believers, when they find out that they are hypocrites and treat them like the world does then they start to lose faith in God.

Frustrated and wounded leadership

I don't believe that most of the leaders in the stories above want to hurt anyone, but most of the time they are themselves frustrated because of so many rejections from some members who are truly seriously lacking in character. Because of that they start to apply the same tactic on any believer who approaches them with similar symptoms. We know that rejection is a serious problem for anyone and especially for leaders. However we must all be "overcomers" and bounce back and treat every individual with respect, discern the spirit behind the individual and correct or nurture them appropriately. We must learn the skill of spiritual agility; we need to recognize the enemy's work, since we do not wrestle against flesh and blood but against evil spirit manifesting themselves through people's character.

The faith walk is not just for common believers, it is particularly for leaders who have to deal with different personalities and treat them as God would not out of their wounds but out of the abundant of their heart filled with the Holy Spirit.

I learned that anyone who decides to walk by faith in God will have to fight for it and the type of fight for each individual is different depending on their background and faith level. This clearly supported by Romans 7:31(God's Word translation)

"So I've discovered this truth: Evil is present with me even when I want to do what God's standards say is good".

1 Peter 4:12 says rightfully,

"Beloved, think it not strange concerning the fiery trial which is to try you, as though some strange thing happened unto you:"

When we are walking by faith, we must fight because the enemy is trying to stop us from succeeding in that walk. He will bring strange things to cause us to turn from our faith walk.

Pressing toward the mark in the mist of adversity

Brother Jonas was a very eloquent brother in the Lord. He was married to a wonderful Christian lady who is one of the ministers of their church. Brother Jonas has a drug addiction problem that takes him away from home periodically which seriously affects his career and ability to provide for his family. Brother Jonas took some ministry classes that he passed with honor however because of the addiction problem he was not able to reach the ministry position in his local church. However he was faithful to go on the street and minister to people who were in drug rehabilitation center and was very successful doing so but his church never recognized that work.

A few years ago Brother Jonas passed away and was fully honored by those who received his ministry while his church was still talking about his shortcoming.

Brother Jonas did not give up in pursuing the call to evangelize in his life even though his church family denied him that call by refusing to ordain him because of his addiction issues. He has surely fought and won the good fight of faith, thank God that those he ministered to testified on his behalf.

Unbelieving response from a homeless family

Brother Darryl and Sister Tasha have been both raised in Christian families. They knew each other since high school and finally got married after sister Tasha had two daughters during her first marriage that did not work out. They both know the Scripture however she has a very strong domineering, manipulative and controlling spirit while he seems nice from his own perspective and the way he display his love is to let her have her way all the time. This situation went on for about ten years of their marriage during which Darryl was making steady income and providing for his family. However He started to experience job losses due to some complication concerning his work license; his salary was drastically reduced and lost his home an were on the street sleeping in their car with a seven years old son and a three years old granddaughter.

A church family friend of theirs learned about their situation and had compassion on them and took them under their own roof for four months so that they can save enough to rent a place to live, free of charge. Furthermore after the four months, the compassionate family allowed them to occupy their rental house and take over the rent until the end of the lease which Darryl's family was happy to do. However Darryl never paid a single full month rent for three months always coming up with some out of this world kind of excuses. Finally the compassionate family has to ask them to go rent a place they can afford which they agreed to do but were still secretly and illegally occupying the rental house. Furthermore to prevent the compassionate family from entering their own rental house, they disabled the garage door from inside and placed furniture on the main door to prevent them from opening it.

Ungodly pastoral counseling

Pastor Papella counseled the wife to leave her husband because he said the husband is hardheaded and does not listen to him. The question is what is the basis of this counseling? Is it Biblical or is it human wisdom? I think it is human wisdom therefore not appropriate.

A Cracked Foundation

Why do some Christians and most of us do not really believe? Most Christians who would read that question will be offended for even saying that some Christian believers really do not believe in what Jesus said. When this happens, we need to seriously check our foundation. As a biblical example we know that Abraham's father was an idol worshipper:

Then Joshua gathered all the tribes of Israel to Shechem and called for the elders of Israel, for their heads, for their judges, and for their officers; and they presented themselves before God. And Joshua said to all the people, "Thus says the LORD God of Israel: 'Your fathers, including Terah, the father of Abraham and the father of Nahor, dwelt on the other side of the River[a] in old times; and they served other gods. Then I took your father Abraham from the other side of the River, led him throughout all the land of Canaan, and multiplied his descendants and gave him Isaac. Joshua 24:1-3

Before each one of us believers was saved, we or our forefathers were serving other gods. Jesus came so that He can reconcile us back to the Father and the true foundation which is Christ Jesus. If we do not really believe then our Christian foundation is cracked. And when the foundation of a building is cracked it open doors to all types of elements and creatures to attack and take down the building.

Our True Spiritual Foundation:

We believers in the Body of Christ are part of a building that is being built by God and not men:

for he waited for the city which has foundations, whose builder and maker is God. Hebrews 11:10

That building requires a solid foundation and that foundation is Jesus Christ:

For no other foundation can anyone lay than that which is laid, which is Jesus Christ. 1 Corinthians 3:11

God has hired builders in the form of His called and ordained leading ministers: Apostles, Prophets, Evangelists, Pastors and Teachers:

having been built on the foundation of the apostles and prophets, Jesus Christ Himself being the chief cornerstone, Ephesians 2:20

And He Himself gave some to be apostles, some prophets, some evangelists, and some pastors and teachers, for the equipping of the saints for the work of ministry, for the edifying of the body of Christ. Ephesians 4:11

If one becomes a believers in Christ, he/she lays his/her foundation on the True foundation which is Christ Jesus, so if that person backslides it is as if he/she lays a foundation but did not persevere to build his spiritual life on it. The enemy will be happy because the person did not continue to grow in Christ.

lest, after he has laid the foundation, and is not able to finish, all who see it begin to mock him, Luke 14:29

It is a distrustful thing to start laying a foundation on the True foundation and then turn back, it is as if we do not really believe:

Still another said, "I will follow you, Lord; but first let me go back and say goodbye to my family." Jesus replied, "No one who puts a hand to the plow and looks back is fit for service in the kingdom of God." Luke 9:61-62

In the above passage Jesus rebuke the disciple who wanted to take care of his family before coming to serve Him because that statement reveals his true foundation which is a cracked foundation, so the Lord used this sharp rebuke to correct that foundation.

In fact in Genesis 12:1 God was showing how important it is to set that foundation straight:

Now the LORD had said to Abram:

"Get out of your country,

From your family

And from your father's house,

To a land that I will show you. Genesis 12:1

Therefore for us to restore our foundation we first need to remove the defective foundation: Abraham father is an idol worshipper:

Then Joshua gathered all the tribes of Israel to Shechem and called for the elders of Israel, for their heads, for their judges, and for their officers; and they presented themselves before God. And Joshua said to all the people, "Thus says the LORD God of Israel: 'Your fathers, including Terah, the father of Abraham and the father of Nahor, dwelt on the other side of the River[a] in old times; and they served other gods. Then I took your father Abraham from the other side of the River, led him throughout all the land of Canaan, and multiplied his descendants and gave him Isaac. Joshua 24:1-3

Because of that God gave Abraham the command to get out of his country, out of his family and out of his father (Terah)'s house because they served other gods and not the true God. Abraham who was chosen by the True God has to require separation from Abraham's native country and family tradition and from the idol worship environment because the environment in which we live shapes us.

This is the model of faith I believe God is calling us all to follow when He call us to salvation in Jesus Christ. So when we are saved we must (1) leave "our country", (2) leave "our people", (3) leave our "father's household" and (4) go to follow Jesus that we do not see.

Why do we have to leave our country when God calls us to salvation?

The understanding is not that we have to physically leave our native country – because we are in the world but not part of the world - but that we have to first identify ourselves as people of God before where we come from. Each country is ruled by natural as well as physical authorities who have established soul ties with all who live in the land. Because most people come from a non Christian background, they need to break from those ties to be able to be fully free to walk in faith in God.

Why do we have to leave our people when God calls us to salvation?

Again we are not necessarily talking about physically leaving our people but the Bible commands us to come out of their evil practices if we want to really walk by faith in God. If we do not break that tie, we will be seriously hindered in our walk of faith in God. For example if we know that an established tradition is not rooted in God and we are blindly following it them we can be deceived and the enemy can use it as a stronghold in our lives.

Why do we have to leave our father's household when God calls us to salvation?

We have to leave our father's house because God wants to give us a new vision of where he wants us to go. Usually the parents have their vision of the child's life that does not necessarily align with God's plan for the child; particularly when the parents are idol worshippers and witches. Also the parental tie is very strong and if the parents are ungodly they will have strong generation bondage for the children to break. Therefore when we are saved we must break from ungodly parental ties.

This is also true for a church and its members. When believers in a church become mature they must be released into their ministries that God has called them to carry on. Sometimes it may involve physically leaving the church to create another or a ministry particularly when the local church is not known to let people go. Any attempt to control individual destinies will lead to the purpose of God in the lives of those individuals being delayed or aborted.

We have faith in God and fight for our faith because what God has done and continues to do from Genesis to Revelation is clearly revealed and represents solid basis for our hope and love in Him.

Unbelief is a cancer in the church because it causes the believer to displease God because unbelief. Hebrews 11:6 says *"But without faith it is impossible to please him: for he that cometh to God must believe that he is, and that he is a rewarder of them that diligently seek him."* Everyone is subject to the frantic attacks of the enemy on the mind to cause us to disbelieve. Therefore we will often find ourselves face to face with situations that challenge our faith in such a way that we doubt what God has clearly said. When the failures multiply they lead to discouragement and disbelief. The goal of the enemy is to steal God's perspective of the problem from us so that we will believe a lie rather than the truth of the All Mighty Creator of all that exist.

But thank be to God that He is a forgiving God and give us grace to repent and keep fighting. O brothers and sisters in the Lord of Lord and King of kings, let's wake up from our spiritual sleep because hell is real, and do what the Lord has saved us to do, to set captives walking to the pit free, by believing in Jesus and breaking away from world system in the image of Sodom and of Gomorrah multiplied.

Chapter Four: Warnings from Biblical Prophecy

Granted. But they were broken off because of unbelief, and you stand by faith. Do not be arrogant, but tremble. Romans 11:20

The question is why is it that most would rather believe a lie when challenged with an issue in which God has already declared us victorious? I believe the answer lies in self preservation which is rooted in fear of men and fear of death or hurt.

The Word of God warns us time and time again that unbelief which rooted in lack of faith in God has devastating consequences. When a person does not believe anything is open for that person and since the wages of sin is death the unbeliever has chosen his course already. Because believe or not the same consequence is unavoidable which is the wages of sin is death:

The wages of the righteous is life, but the earnings of the wicked are sin and death. Proverbs 10:16

For the wages of sin is death, but the gift of God is eternal life in Christ Jesus our Lord. Romans 6:23

The consequences of unbelief is severe, some will not be allowed to enter the Kingdom of God because of unbelief:

So we see that they were not able to enter, because of their unbelief. Hebrews 3:19

We believe by the grace of God, so if we keep on not believing then we have not received grace. A believer who has truly received the grace of God will believe and will not continue in unbelief:

No! We believe it is through the grace of our Lord Jesus that we are saved, just as they are." Acts 15:11

When Apollos wanted to go to Achaia, the brothers and sisters encouraged him and wrote to the disciples there to welcome him. When he arrived, he was a great help to those who by grace had believed. Acts 18:27

He has saved us and called us to a holy life—not because of anything we have done but because of his own purpose and grace. This grace was given us in Christ Jesus before the beginning of time, 2 Timothy 1:9

God's Grace gives us another chance to make it right when we sin because we live in a fallen world where the enemy has many venues to tempt us, but it is not for us to continue sinning and boldly standing in unbelief and expect grace to bail us out. We need to get to a point when we feel deep sorrow when we realize we have sinned against God and not have the attitude that "I can keep on sinning because grace will pick me up".

Here what the Apostle John teaches us about a person who continues to sin:

And now, dear children, continue in him, so that when he appears we may be confident and unashamed before him at his coming. 1 John 2:28

No one who is born of God will continue to sin, because God's seed remains in them; they cannot go on sinning, because they have been born of God. 1 John 3:9

We know that anyone born of God does not continue to sin; the One who was born of God keeps them safe, and the evil one cannot harm them. 1 John 5:18

We should rather examine ourselves daily and see if we are continuing on a path of sin, if we realize we are then we must repent and ask the Holy Spirit to help us remain in God's will and never go back to that sin again. We should never be complacent with sin because God is very serious about sin.

Root Source of unbelief: darkness in the world

We are called out of darkness and from a dark world we live in. We live in a dangerous land covered with evil spirits influencing or directly using people to attack our faith in God by all means necessary.

"Arise, shine, for your light has come,

and the glory of the LORD rises upon you.

See, darkness covers the earth

and thick darkness is over the peoples,

but the LORD rises upon you

and his glory appears over you.

Nations will come to your light,

and kings to the brightness of your dawn. Isaiah 60:1-3

The life on earth is like a people living in captivity, under a wicked kingdom who is trying to kill, steal and destroy the believer and the creation of God. In the Bible this is like the time of Daniel and his friends as well as the people of Israel living in a land of captivity in Babylon. Thank God that He is in control of all things so that Daniel and his friends can stand firm in their faith in Him and shine through that dark kingdom.

Looking at the seven churches of Revelation as pictures of the fight of faith

We look at the Lord's letter to the seven churches as some type of report card for the level of faith in Him. Being the Author and Finisher of our faith, the Lord

Jesus measures the faith level of the seven churches based on their habits and revealed heart. For this reason the Lord repeats the phrase "him that has an ear let him hear", we know that "faith comes by hearing" the Word of God, those who hear, increase in faith, repent and are restored. But there is a warning of destruction for those who continue in the dead paths. The Lord Jesus was the Seed that was sowed in the world, a seed is supposed to produce the crop for which the one who sowed purposed. He sowed so that we can reap faith in Him. But if our lives do not show evidence of walking by faith in Him we must repent. The seven churches are historic as well as prophetic churches; therefore even today we have these types of churches showing the condition of our fighting the good fight of faith:

The typical Ephesus church based on Rev. 2:1-7:

The typical Ephesus church is a church which shows excellence in external work and dedication for the Lord but has left the "First Love" which is Jesus. In these churches they have departed from the truth of the Gospel and faith in God to a certain degree, counting on what they can achieve in the natural based on intellect and financial resources. Jesus warns to repent and come back to Him. A true believer must let him or herself be led by the Holy Spirit in every area of life, even the use of our mental faculties must be submitted to the Holy Spirit in order to produce good works otherwise we will be producing dead works whatever area we are operating, this even applies to the work of the ministry. Every ministry that originates from the mind of the man and not from the Spirit is actually a curse. It is a curse because we think we can help God instead of us asking God to do it through us. It is a curse because we have chosen to eat from the tree of the knowledge of good and evil, we are our own master. We were created to eat from the Tree of Life meaning under the complete dependence on the Holy Spirit for every area of life and for everything.

The typical Smyrna church based on Rev. 2:8-11:

The typical Smyrna church is a church who undergoes persecution and material lacks in the present and even more in the future but remains faithful to the Gospel of Jesus Christ even to death. The Lord encourages them to continue to be faithful to the end and not depart from the faith. This is a category of churches that is winning the good fight of faith.

The typical Smyrna church is therefore at the front line of the good fight of faith because they constantly stand for their faith in God in the face of persecution. The most powerful enemy is discouragement, if they are discouraged they will start to hate God for allowing them to suffer that's why the Lord commands them to continue to fight the good fight of faith and not get weary.

The typical Pergamum church based on Rev. 2:12-17:

The typical Pergamum church is a church that remains true to the Name of the Lord even in an environment where Satan is ruling, however they have allowed themselves to receive corrupted doctrines or doctrines of demons that enslave some in immorality and apostasy.

The typical Thyatira church based on Rev. 2:1-7:

The typical Thyatira church is a church that tolerates the spirit of Jezebel which is rebellion, adultery and witchcraft spirit deceiving God's true servant into sexual immorality and idolatry. This is a church that the enemy has strong influence on, causing people to depart from the Gospel of Jesus Christ.

The typical Sardis church based on Rev. 3:1-6:

The typical Sardis church is a church showing externally to be very alive but in fact is spiritually dead because they rely more on other things than on the Gospel of Christ. The devil has been successful deceiving them in thinking that the external show of liveliness is the work of God but in fact it is not. It is a dying church and must repent and come back to the faith in God.

The typical Philadelphia church based on Rev. 2:7-13:

The typical Philadelphia church is a church that is doing good work – compared to dead work - walking in faith in God and fighting the good fight of faith, they have kept the Lord's command and patiently endured the consequences. The Lord compliments them and tells them to hold on to that faith and not give up. This is another category of churches that is winning the good fight of faith.

The typical Laodicea church based on Rev. 2:14-22:

The typical Laodicea church is a church without spine, immature in the faith because she allows herself to be tossed around without any firm belief in what is true. She is likely to be tolerant of all kinds of other faiths without discernment. Her faith is shaky but she thinks that because of her great material wealth and possessions and probably intellectual abilities, she is rich but in fact she is spiritually bankrupt.

These seven churches are seen from God's perspective and give us what a church that is fighting the good fight of faith should or should not look like. It is a picture that God want us to see in order to repent when we momentarily lose the fight of faith and return to Him.

This chapter was purposed to present various evidence of the fight for our faith that is taking place at every single area of our lives at the individual level as well as at the corporate Christian community levels. The statistics can only show the tip of the iceberg, but we need to understand that our walk of faith will be opposed at every level of our life on earth. The fight for our faith is a real battle, a spiritual battle having implications on every aspect of our life.

2 Thessalonians 2:3 says *"Let no man deceive you by any means: for that day shall not come, except there come a falling away first, and that man of sin be revealed, the son of perdition;"* We believe the falling away that will take place in the last days is the loss of faith in God by the great majority of people including believers who "have a form of godliness" but deny the power of God, or those believer who think they are rich in the natural but really very poor in the spiritual, those who are not able to stand for what they believe or those who rely on their own abilities instead of on God in achieving God's purpose.

Since faith is the only way we can receive anything from God, the devil concentrates his attacks on our faith by deceptive tactics so that we would lose faith and have fear instead or putting our faith in him or in ourselves instead of in God alone.

Jesus is coming back for His holy people not those who do not really believe in Him

Believers must stop guessing and second guessing God. This is not a joke, life is not a joke, what we do on earth have eternal consequences on where we spend eternity.

For those still doubting here a few biblical revelations:

There is a heaven but there a hell also

Therefore any doctrine that waters down the message of hell and trivializes it is a doctrine of demons. Any doctrine that tries to demonstrate that hell does not exist by emphasizing the love of God is also a doctrine of demons because it gives carnal believers a reason to stay warm and not have the fear of the Lord because they reason in their hear that hell does not exist or is not literal.

God does not lie

Therefore God is not bluffing when His Word warns us of eternal damnation in hell. The following are the very words of Jesus Christ our Lord to help those who still trust in their pet doctrines more than the teaching of Jesus have a holy fear of God: this matter very seriously and

But the subjects of the kingdom will be thrown outside, into the darkness, where there will be weeping and gnashing of teeth." Matthew 8:12

They will throw them into the blazing furnace, where there will be weeping and gnashing of teeth. Matthew 13:42

and throw them into the blazing furnace, where there will be weeping and gnashing of teeth. Matthew 13:50

"Then the king told the attendants, 'Tie him hand and foot, and throw him outside, into the darkness, where there will be weeping and gnashing of teeth.' Matthew 22:13

He will cut him to pieces and assign him a place with the hypocrites, where there will be weeping and gnashing of teeth. Matthew 24:51

And throw that worthless servant outside, into the darkness, where there will be weeping and gnashing of teeth.' Matthew 25:30

"There will be weeping there, and gnashing of teeth, when you see Abraham, Isaac and Jacob and all the prophets in the kingdom of God, but you yourselves thrown out. Luke 13:28

One thing is to understand that there is a hell another is to know some of the things that a believer does of fails to do that can take that believer to hell. Meditate on each of the reasons Jesus mentioned in the passages of Scriptures above why the people ended up in hell.

God still hates sin and the wages of sin is death

God the Father allowed His own Son Jesus to be tortured and brutally killed because of sin proving that God is very serious about sin.

This truth has not changed, grace does not mean that God tolerate sin:

"For the wages of sin is death, but the gift of God is eternal life in[a] Christ Jesus our Lord." Romans 6:23-24

Is life worth the gamble?

It may be OK to gamble with this life because one can die and end the suffering but it is unconceivable to gamble with once eternal destiny because there is no end in the suffering in hell just as there is no end in the joy in Heaven.

Jesus is still coming back for His holy people not those who are not ready

Jesus is not coming back for people who are not ready, He is coming back for a holy people:

Know ye not that the unrighteous shall not inherit the kingdom of God? Be not deceived: neither fornicators, nor idolaters, nor adulterers, nor effeminate, nor abusers of themselves with mankind, 1 Corinthians 6:9

Envyings, murders, drunkenness, revellings, and such like: of the which I tell you before, as I have also told you in time past, that they which do such things shall not inherit the kingdom of God. Galatians 5:21

And the very God of peace sanctify you wholly; and I pray God your whole spirit and soul and body be preserved blameless unto the coming of our Lord Jesus Christ. 1 Thessalonians 5:23

Those who are not ready will remain behind. Those believers who will remain behind will look like the following at the least prior to the coming:

Know ye not that the unrighteous shall not inherit the kingdom of God? Be not deceived: neither fornicators, nor idolaters, nor adulterers, nor effeminate, nor abusers of themselves with mankind, 1 Corinthians 6:9

Envyings, murders, drunkenness, revellings, and such like: of the which I tell you before, as I have also told you in time past, that they which do such things shall not inherit the kingdom of God. Galatians 5:21

The hard truth

The following passages of the Bible give the hard truth about who is and is not Christian. This is not to condemn but to warm the living so that they will repent and come to Jesus:

We know that we have passed from death to life, because we love each other. Anyone who does not love remains in death. 1 John 3:14

Dear children, let us not love with words or speech but with actions and in truth. 1 John 3:18

Whoever does not love does not know God, because God is love. 1 John 4:8

Whoever claims to love God yet hates a brother or sister is a liar. For whoever does not love their brother and sister, whom they have seen, cannot love God, whom they have not seen 1 John 4:20

We need to deeply meditate on these passages of Scripture and examine ourselves to see if we have failed in this area and repent and ask the Holy Spirit to help us remain in God's will.

O Lord Jesus deliver us from evil, for many of us are sleeping and are made dull in getting understanding. Deliver us from unbelief and set us free to worship you in spirit and in truth. We choose to follow you, to abide in you just as Abraham remained with you and pleaded that you spear the righteous in Sodom and Gomorrah. Deliver your people who have been taken captive in this world system and set us free to do your will and to walk by faith all the days of our lives.

Chapter Five: The Cancer of Unbelief in A Christian's Life

From him the whole body, joined and held together by every supporting ligament, grows and builds itself up in love, as each part does its work.
Ephesians 4:15

We are called into one Body, the Body of Christ. If we do not want the Body to suffer the effect of Cancer, we all come to the source of Life which is Jesus Christ. By allowing unbelief and lack of faith in the Christian community, we allow Cancer to attack the Body. We know that Cancer can never kill the Body of Christ but for some generations, it may be crippled by that disease.

What are some of the manifestations of the Cancer in the Body?

Whatever cause division in the Body of Christ is not from God. The source of denominational division is not a work of God. Interdenominational turf wars are not from God, these are the manifestation of a spreading Cancer, a work of the fleshly nature of man. There should only be one doctrine, the one taught by Christ summing up both new and old Testaments of the Bible.

Webster's Unabridged Dictionary states in its Biblical definition of believer, that a believer is "*One who gives credit to the truth of the Scriptures, as a revelation from God; a Christian; -- in a more restricted sense, one who receives Christ as his Savior, and accepts the way of salvation unfolded in the gospel.*"

Faith believing is a choice after having been convicted in our heart by the Holy Spirit concerning the Truth of the Gospel, to believe God in Jesus Christ. It is a choice to put away our hesitation and doubt and completely trust God for what He said. If we are believers in Christ then we have to receive without any hint of doubt what Jesus taught us and what the Spirit of God uses people of God to teach us. Either we believe or we don't because we cannot eat of the tree of life (life submitted totally to the Holy Spirit) and also eat from the tree of knowledge of good and evil (a self driven life). The first way of life enthrones God in one's life while the second way of life enthrones self. I believe unbelief is the result of enthroning self rather than enthroning God in our Christian life.

The Bible clearly says that when we completely surrender our lives to God He will keep and lead us in all our ways so that we will walk in victory no matter the circumstances. The challenge of the Christian, the fight of faith is to trust God to let our lives be led by Him because we are constantly bombarded with temptations designed to distract us from our walk of faith.

The devil introduced the self driven life in the Garden of Eden by deceiving Adam and Eve:

Now the LORD God had planted a garden in the east, in Eden; and there he put the man he had formed. The LORD God made all kinds of trees grow out of the ground—trees that were pleasing to the eye and good for food. In the middle of the garden were the tree of life and the tree of the knowledge of good and evil. Genesis 2:8-9

The LORD God made garments of skin for Adam and his wife and clothed them. And the LORD God said, "The man has now become like one of us, knowing good and evil. He must not be allowed to reach out his hand and take also from the tree of life and eat, and live forever." So the LORD God banished him from the Garden of Eden to work the ground from which he had been taken. Genesis 3:21-23

Once we choose to eat from the tree of knowledge of good and evil we are no longer allowed to eat from the tree of life. We can only eat from one at a time; we cannot have both at one time. In other words either we choose to believe God and obey all what He says or we choose not to believe what God says and believe in ourselves, our understanding, our intellect, our pet doctrine etc...Ether we choose to receive revelations or we choose to increase knowledge in order to rule our own lives. There is nothing wrong in increasing knowledge but what makes the difference is the driving force of that knowledge increase. If the knowledge increase is prompted by God who is leading a believer then it is good but if that person is seeking to increase for self aggrandizement then it is a tree of knowledge of good and evil to promote self effort.

When we choose our own ways we are cursed because we have to work hard to live since we will be "kicked out of the Garden of Eden"

The Word of God is our lamp to get us back into the Spirit when we fall out of it, it is a school master to teach and train us when we are young in the faith. But we must grow in Christ to a point where we can be sensitive to the Holy Spirit that was sealed to us in the day of redemption to teach us all things and the Spirit and the written Word of God always agree.

Some Powerful weapons in the enemy's arsenal to be aware of

Unbelief has sisters and brothers, they are: discouragement, fear of the enemy and of man, selfishness, pride, etc...

Many weapons the enemy uses are abstract in the sense that we don't realize we have been attacked while under intense fire. But one thing that is important to note is that they are destined to negatively affect our heart and our faith in God. Many times the Lord Jesus repeated "fear not", "do not be afraid", "let not your heart be troubled" etc... because these will affect our heart:

Keep your heart with all diligence,

    For out of it spring the issues of life. Proverbs 4:23

Therefore it is extremely important for a believer to keep a pure heart, a heart that is not pure is vulnerable to the enemy's attacks, that's why Matthew 5:8 teaches us:

Blessed are the pure in heart,

For they shall see God.

We must understand the goal of the enemy, it is to kill, to steal and to destroy (John 10:10) and any weapon that can affect our heart – which is our spirit – can be very effective against us. Keeping a pure heart is the most effective defensive weapon we have when he attacks our heart. Keeping a pure heart is a decision to obey God in any circumstance. This is only possible with the help of the Holy Spirit our helper who is given to us believers in the day of redemption. The following are some of the most dangerous weapons of the enemy against our heart:

Discouragement

Walking by faith require great courage. Discouragement comes when we accept the version of truth of the enemy which is always a lie or a deceptive way of presenting reality for the sole purpose to kill, to steal and to destroy, rather than the perspective of God. When we are discouraged we give up our spiritual authority over the devil and his agents who will surely use it to attack us. When we are discouraged we accept defeat in the place of the God promised victory over every circumstance. Biblical records shows that God repeatedly encouraged his people and his called ministers, some of those are:

God Repeatedly Encouraged Israel:

Be strong and courageous. Do not be afraid or terrified because of them, for the LORD your God goes with you; he will never leave you nor forsake you." Deuteronomy 31:6

Then Moses summoned Joshua and said to him in the presence of all Israel, "Be strong and courageous, for you must go with this people into the land that the LORD swore to their ancestors to give them, and you must divide it among them as their inheritance. Deuteronomy 31:7

The LORD gave this command to Joshua son of Nun: "Be strong and courageous, for you will bring the Israelites into the land I promised them on oath, and I myself will be with you." Deuteronomy 31:23

Then you will have success if you are careful to observe the decrees and laws that the LORD gave Moses for Israel. Be strong and courageous. Do not be afraid or discouraged. 1 Chronicles 22:13

"Be strong and courageous. Do not be afraid or discouraged because of the king of Assyria and the vast army with him, for there is a greater power with us than with him. 2 Chronicles 32:7

David Encouraged Solomon

David also said to Solomon his son, "Be strong and courageous, and do the work. Do not be afraid or discouraged, for the LORD God, my God, is with you. He will not fail you or forsake you until all the work for the service of the temple of the LORD is finished. 1 Chronicles 28:20

God Repeatedly Encouraged Joshua

Be strong and courageous, because you will lead these people to inherit the land I swore to their ancestors to give them. Joshua 1:6

"Be strong and very courageous. Be careful to obey all the law my servant Moses gave you; do not turn from it to the right or to the left, that you may be successful wherever you go. Joshua 1:7

Have I not commanded you? Be strong and courageous. Do not be afraid; do not be discouraged, for the LORD your God will be with you wherever you go." Joshua 1:9

Whoever rebels against your word and does not obey it, whatever you may command them, will be put to death. Only be strong and courageous!" Joshua 1:18

Joshua said to them, "Do not be afraid; do not be discouraged. Be strong and courageous. This is what the LORD will do to all the enemies you are going to fight." Joshua 10:25

Be on your guard; stand firm in the faith; be courageous; be strong. 1 Corinthians 16:13

Fear

Fear is the weapon of the enemy against our faith in God. Fear is of the devil because

There is no fear in love; but perfect love casts out fear, because fear involves torment. But he who fears has not been made perfect in love. 1 John 4:18.

Because God does not torment us, fear does not come from God. Fear is an indication of our level of love. God did not give us the spirit of fear therefore we know that fear is not of God:

For God hath not given us the spirit of fear; but of power, and of love, and of a sound mind. 2 Timothy 1:7

Instead God commends us to have no fear at all of anything or any man:

Fear thou not; for I am with thee: be not dismayed; for I am thy God: I will strengthen thee; yea, I will help thee; yea, I will uphold thee with the right hand of my righteousness Isaiah 41:10

The only kind of fear that is healthy is the fear of God that will deter us from sinning against Him:

The fear of the LORD is the beginning of wisdom; A good understanding have all those who do His commandments. His praise endures forever. Psalm 111:10

The fear of the LORD is the beginning of knowledge, But fools despise wisdom and instruction. 2.Proverbs 1:7

" *The fear of the LORD is the beginning of wisdom, And the knowledge of the Holy One is understanding.* Proverbs 9:10

Solomon concluded the following that sums it up:

Let us hear the conclusion of the whole matter: Fear God and keep His commandments,

For this is man's all. Ecclesiastes 12:13

The fear of the enemy brings a snare while the fear of the Lord liberates. Proverbs 29:25 says: *The fear of man brings a snare, But whoever trusts in the LORD shall be safe.*

Selfishness

God did not create us to be self sufficient; He created us to be interdependent working in harmony, just like all the cells in a human body working together to make a human life possible every day. We are created as living cells in the Body of Christ to build it up in love.

Now the works of the flesh are evident, which are: adultery,[c] fornication, uncleanness, lewdness, idolatry, sorcery, hatred, contentions, jealousies, outbursts of wrath, selfish ambitions, dissensions, heresies, envy, murders,[d] drunkenness, revelries, and the like; of which I tell you beforehand, just as I also told you in time past, that those who practice such things will not inherit the kingdom of God. Galatians 5:19-21

Pride

Pride goes before destruction, And a haughty spirit before a fall. Proverbs 16:18

Before destruction the heart of a man is haughty, And before honor is humility. Proverbs 18:12

The Plan of God for the Development of the Body of Christ (Ephesians 4:1-16)

The following passage of Scripture is a great summary of the vision and purpose of the Body:

As a prisoner for the Lord, then, I urge you to live a life worthy of the calling you have received. Be completely humble and gentle; be patient, bearing with one another in love. Make every effort to keep the unity of the Spirit through the bond of peace. There is one body and one Spirit, just as you were called to one hope when you were called; one Lord, one faith, one baptism; one God and Father of all, who is over all and through all and in all. But to each one of us grace has been given as Christ apportioned it. This is why it[a] says:

"When he ascended on high,

he took many captives

and gave gifts to his people."[b]

(What does "he ascended" mean except that he also descended to the lower, earthly regions[c]? He who descended is the very one who ascended higher than all the heavens, in order to fill the whole universe.) So Christ himself gave the apostles, the prophets, the evangelists, the pastors and teachers, to equip his people for works of service, so that the body of Christ may be built up until we all reach unity in the faith and in the knowledge of the Son of God and become mature, attaining to the whole measure of the fullness of Christ.

Then we will no longer be infants, tossed back and forth by the waves, and blown here and there by every wind of teaching and by the cunning and craftiness of people in their deceitful scheming. Instead, speaking the truth in love, we will grow to become in every respect the mature body of him who is the head, that is, Christ. From him the whole body, joined and held together by every supporting ligament, grows and builds itself up in love, as each part does its work. Ephesians 4:1-16

This passage teaches us that there is one God and there is no reason for division, it also teaches us that the Christian life is a process that needs to reach maturity. It tells us how the members of the Body are supposed to function to reach the goal of fully building up the Body *"until we all reach unity in the faith and in the knowledge of the Son of God and become mature, attaining to the whole measure of the fullness of Christ."* There are categories of leading agents in the process (apostles, prophets, evangelists, pastors and teachers) and their job is *"to equip his people for works of service, so that the body of Christ may be built up until we all reach unity in the faith and in the knowledge of the Son of God and become mature, attaining to the whole measure of the fullness of Christ. "* The work of the ministry is not just for some few gurus but for all the people who believe. This passage also teaches that we are to grow up and not remain infants and what would constitute signs of maturity:

Then we will no longer be infants, tossed back and forth by the waves, and blown here and there by every wind of teaching and by the cunning and craftiness of people in their deceitful scheming. Instead, speaking the truth in love, we will grow to become in every respect the mature body of him who is the head, that is, Christ.

The sign of a mature Christian is not how a person can play church of show they are religious but how they react to various conflicting doctrines of men. They are unmovable because they have faith in the Truth, Jesus Christ and nothing can move them from that position. The mature Christian speaks the truth in love and not hate nor apathy.

Why does the enemy work so hard to stop that growth to maturity? Because when the Body is folly grown and each believer is truly grounded in Christ, the enemy cannot freely do what he wants. One of the weapons he uses to attack the Body is unbelief and lack of faith so as to cause a Cancer in the Body.

Unbelief is lethal to the Body, it limits or eliminates a person's inner ability to accomplish a vision. It robs the believer of his authority in Christ because we cannot receive any spiritual thing if we do not believe. Unbelief is spiritual poverty, as faith is spiritual riches, for without faith we cannot please God. Even Jesus did not freely do His work where the unbelief was so strong:

Now He did not do many mighty works there because of their unbelief. Matthew 13:58

And He marveled because of their unbelief. Then He went about the villages in a circuit, teaching. Mark 6:6

Jesus rebukes His disciples every time they moved in unbelief:

Later He appeared to the eleven as they sat at the table; and He rebuked their unbelief and hardness of heart, because they did not believe those who had seen Him after He had risen. Mark 16:14

God harshly deal with His people when they move in unbelief:

Well said. Because of unbelief they were broken off, and you stand by faith. Do not be haughty, but fear. Romans 11:20

So we see that they could not enter in because of unbelief. Hebrews 3:19

God can forgive us when we move in unbelief but ignorantly:

although I was formerly a blasphemer, a persecutor, and an insolent man; but I obtained mercy because I did it ignorantly in unbelief. 1 Timothy 1:13

Believer must believe, we must stand on the foundation of Jesus Christ and be unmovable or we will become useless for good work and full of "Cancer" because we will become ineffective in accomplishing what God has called to accomplish

Chapter Six : Identifying and Uprooting the Strongman

Or how can one enter a strong man's house and plunder his goods, unless he first binds the strong man? And then he will plunder his house. Matthew 12:29

Why is it that dream that we have of our lives encounters obstacles? Why is it that when we want to do good there is opposition of all sorts? Why is it that when one wants to help people in needs the very people who should be thankful are the very one who attack your motives and your character? Why is it that a poor country that has been in colonized and becomes independent for fifty years, wanting to finally autonomously run its own destiny is faced with overwhelming war with overwhelming weaponry and the whole world watches with apathy? Why is it that those parents who want to do the right things by raising their children in the fear and admonition of the Lord are faced with legal suit because their children mentioned the Name of Jesus in school and want to express their faith? Why is it that a God fearing husband who wants to lead his family as God instructs it is continually faced with disrespect and defiance at home thwarting every godly initiative? Why is it that a God fearing woman wanting to submit to her husband as the Lord instructed is met with physical abuses? Why is it that a believer wanting to believe literally what the Word of God says and aligning his life and ministry on it, is met with criticism from religious leaders?

Why is it that every decision we make in life is opposed from likely as well as unlikely sources? These questions attempt to uncover something that believers – or anyone for that matter – faces. It seems as though there was an invisible barrier that works very hard to stop anyone from doing what God's will is, from doing the right thing, for reaching a godly goal.

A clear example of this can be directly observed in the life of a pastor who truly wants to help the people of God grow in grace. Anyone who has been close to a pastor's life can testify what type of challenges a pastor or minister of the Gospel faces every single day. First from their parents or close family members when he or she decides to move in faith and do as he is convinced of the Word of the Lord to go into ministry. Then from those members he or she pours his or her heart to serve. Then sometimes they face ridicules from the media and even jail time with the government for what the boldly declare from the Word of God.

Any person who has achieved a level of high profile leadership position has faced all kinds of obstacles. By looking at a biography of a historical figure, a person who has impacted generation, we see an array of problems that the person has gone through. Sometimes they lose family members, parent, relatives, and friends. We also see that they have overcome numerous obstacles that suddenly appear in the path.

To understand this one must first know that a life that sets as a goal to please God is an uphill battle and to each area of life there is a strongman assigned by the enemy who's sole objective is to thwart the plan of God that the believer has engaged in.

What is a strongman?

A strongman can be an institution, a condition, a relationship, a person or anything which's actions is strategically positioned - knowingly or unknowingly – in a believer's or dreamer's life to stop the progress of the fulfillment of the vision.

An excellent example of a strongman can be found in the Biblical character of Goliath. The story is found in 1 Samuel 17. The following two verses give a brief synopsis of the strongman and his objective:

A champion named Goliath, who was from Gath, came out of the Philistine camp. His height was six cubits and a span. 1 Samuel 17:4

Goliath stood and shouted to the ranks of Israel, "Why do you come out and line up for battle? Am I not a Philistine, and are you not the servants of Saul? Choose a man and have him come down to me. 1 Samuel 17:8

As he was talking with them, Goliath, the Philistine champion from Gath, stepped out from his lines and shouted his usual defiance, and David heard it. 1 Samuel 17:23

The strongman appears to be a very powerful enemy of progress with overwhelming intimidating power. He is persistent to stop the believer in his path to possessing what God has given him to possess.

How strongmen occupied our God given land?

Going back to the original sin of Adam, we understand that sin entered the world and the devil's kingdom got consolidated on the earth. The enemy took over every land that God gave Adam. Consequently every area of life was occupied by the kingdom of darkness:

For the creation was subjected to frustration, not by its own choice, but by the will of the one who subjected it, in hope that[a] the creation itself will be liberated from its bondage to decay and brought into the freedom and glory of the children of God.

We know that the whole creation has been groaning as in the pains of childbirth right up to the present time. Not only so, but we ourselves, who have the firstfruits of the Spirit, groan inwardly as we wait eagerly for our adoption to sonship, the redemption of our bodies. Romans 8:20-23

Because of that occupation, when God says to the children of Israel that He gave them the Promise Land, the actual possessing of the Promise Land was not without battle. The enemy has occupied the land for so long so when the real owners came they have to take out the strongmen of each portion of the land God gave them. There were giants in the land God promised the children of Israel.

Why it is important to fight and uproot the strongman in our "land"?

Our land can be an actual land, but it could also be an area of our lives where there seem to be setbacks, difficulties and obstacles to walking by faith and fulfilling God's promise for our lives.

It is very important that we defeat our strongmen because they are illegally occupying our promised lands. If we are intimidated by them we will surely lose our promised lands:

And they spread among the Israelites a bad report about the land they had explored. They said, "The land we explored devours those living in it. All the people we saw there are of great size. We saw the Nephilim there (the descendants of Anak come from the Nephilim). We seemed like grasshoppers in our own eyes, and we looked the same to them." Numbers 13:32-33

This is a dramatic revelation, we must engage and defeat our strongmen or we will not achieve the purpose God has set before us in our generation.

How to defeat your strongmen

Strongmen hold the keys to possessing our lands. If we do not defeat them we will not be the overcomers God has called us to be, making Him a liar, which does not glorify God in our lives. Israelites who believed the report of the ten spies who went to spy in the land God promised Israel, all died in the wilderness never entering the promise land:

Then Caleb silenced the people before Moses and said, "We should go up and take possession of the land, for we can certainly do it." Numbers 13:30

Joshua son of Nun and Caleb son of Jephunneh, who were among those who had explored the land, tore their clothes Numbers 14:6

But because my servant Caleb has a different spirit and follows me wholeheartedly, I will bring him into the land he went to, and his descendants will inherit it. Numbers 14:24

Not one of you will enter the land I swore with uplifted hand to make your home, except Caleb son of Jephunneh and Joshua son of Nun. Numbers 14:30

This is serious and should motivate all believers to fight the good fight of faith and not bow to intimidation of the enemy.

It is important that we understand that the strongmen of our lives cannot be defeated with human strength or wisdom. It is only by faith in what God can do and will do to the enemy that will give us victory:

Then Moses and Aaron fell facedown in front of the whole Israelite assembly gathered there. Joshua son of Nun and Caleb son of Jephunneh, who were among those who had explored the land, tore their clothes and said to the entire Israelite assembly, "The land we passed through and explored is exceedingly good. If the LORD is pleased with us, he will lead us into that land, a land flowing with milk and honey, and will give it to us. Only do not rebel against the LORD. And do not be afraid of the people of the land, because we will devour them. Their protection is gone, but the LORD is with us. Do not be afraid of them." But the whole assembly talked about stoning them. Then the glory of the LORD appeared at the tent of meeting to all the Israelites. Numbers 14:5-10

Joshua and Caleb believed the report of God and were not intimidated by the giants of the land. For this reason they were the only adults who made it to the land of promise. We should learn this important lesson in our Christian walk. We must trust God to defeat every challenge in our lives, not our own strength or wisdom.

In the defeating of Goliath we also learn how we can defeat our strongmen:

David said to the Philistine, "You come against me with sword and spear and javelin, but I come against you in the name of the LORD Almighty, the God of the armies of Israel, whom you have defied. This day the LORD will deliver you into my hands, and I'll strike you down and cut off your head. This very day I will give the carcasses of the Philistine army to the birds and the wild animals, and the whole world will know that there is a God in Israel. All those gathered here will know that it is not by sword or spear that the LORD saves; for the battle is the LORD's, and he will give all of you into our hands."

As the Philistine moved closer to attack him, David ran quickly toward the battle line to meet him. Reaching into his bag and taking out a stone, he slung it and struck the Philistine on the forehead. The stone sank into his forehead, and he fell facedown on the ground. So David triumphed over the Philistine with a sling and a stone; without a sword in his hand he struck down the Philistine and killed him. David ran and stood over him. He took hold of the Philistine's sword and drew it from the sheath. After he killed him, he cut off his head with the sword. 1 Samuel 17:45-50

David was one man compared to the whole army of Israel intimidated by Goliath, but because He is rooted in his faith in God he was not intimidated and took on Goliath alone and defeated him with a humble weapon giving the glory to God.

The lesson we must learn is that we must believe in God, put our faith in Him and engage the strongmen of our lives. It is not only important for our individual lives but also to the lives of those watching us:

When the Philistines saw that their hero was dead, they turned and ran. Then the men of Israel and Judah surged forward with a shout and pursued the Philistines to the entrance of Gath[f] and to the gates of Ekron. Their dead were strewn along the Shaaraim road to Gath and Ekron. When the Israelites returned from chasing the Philistines, they plundered their camp. 1 Samuel 17:51-53

When we overcome a strongman in our life two great things happen:

First, everything that is associated with that strongmen flee from you because of the victory over the strongman: *When the Philistines saw that their hero was dead, they turned and ran*

Second, the people who are intimidated by that strongman are now fearless because they have been delivered from intimidation: *Then the men of Israel and Judah surged forward with a shout and pursued the Philistines to the entrance of Gath[f] and to the gates of Ekron*

In conclusion, believers must not back down when the Spirit and the Word of God says we must believe the report of the Lord and face every strong man of our life, because the consequences can be disastrous if we don't and God will not get the glory out of our lives. For us to be victorious we must first bind the strong man:

Or how can one enter a strong man's house and plunder his goods, unless he first binds the strong man? And then he will plunder his house. Matthew 12:29

Chapter Seven: Restoring Heart Believing Faith

For God so loved the world that he gave his one and only Son, that whoever believes in him shall not perish but have eternal life. John 3:16

For God did not send his Son into the world to condemn the world, but to save the world through him. Whoever believes in him is not condemned, but whoever does not believe stands condemned already because they have not believed in the name of God's one and only Son. This is the verdict: Light has come into the world, but people loved darkness instead of light because their deeds were evil. John 3:17-19

Jesus replied, "Truly I tell you, if you have faith and do not doubt, not only can you do what was done to the fig tree, but also you can say to this mountain, 'Go, throw yourself into the sea,' and it will be done. If you believe, you will receive whatever you ask for in prayer." Matthew 21:21-23 (NIV)

"Take away the stone," he said. "But, Lord," said Martha, the sister of the dead man, "by this time there is a bad odor, for he has been there four days." Then Jesus said, "Did I not tell you that if you believe, you will see the glory of God?" So they took away the stone. Then Jesus looked up and said, "Father, I thank you that you have heard me. John 11:39-41

The Bible is full of true stories of ordinary people as well as ordinary people called by God to carry on His agenda of that generation. The success stories are always stories of people who fought the good fight of faith in God, sometimes to death. People who believed God and did exactly as God commanded them to do. They were normal people like us but God used them to do His divine work because they did not give up believing God even when sometimes God asked them to do something that did not make sense or even things that appear contrary to who God is. Example God asked Abraham to sacrifice his only (i.e. God promised) son and Abraham believed and was ready to carry it out.

"Jesus said to the people who believed in him, "You are truly my disciples if you remain faithful to my teachings." John 8:31

So it appears the main qualification for being a disciple of Christ is to be faithful to His teachings, to keep having faith in Him. We are also saved by faith alone. Faith in God is a very important requirement for a Christian. Faith is the single most important component of Christianity because without faith we cannot receive from God. By faith we can all things.

Hebrews 11: The "Hall of Faith"

Hebrews 11 clearly teaches us what faith is and what walking by faith should look like.

Hebrews 11 shows us that people God used in the Old Testament were regular people just like us. The only thing that set them apart is that they believed and acted on their belief and what they believed God spoke to them directly.

Verse 32 to 40 states:

" How much more do I need to say? It would take too long to recount the stories of the faith of Gideon, Barak, Samson, Jephthah, David, Samuel, and all the prophets. By faith these people overthrew kingdoms, ruled with justice, and received what God had promised them. They shut the mouths of lions, quenched the flames of fire, and escaped death by the edge of the sword. Their weakness was turned to strength. They became strong in battle and put whole armies to flight. Women received their loved ones back again from death. But others were tortured, refusing to turn from God in order to be set free. They placed their hope in a better life after the resurrection. Some were jeered at, and their backs were cut open with whips. Others were chained in prisons. Some died by stoning, some were sawed in half,[d] and others were killed with the sword. Some went about wearing skins of sheep and goats, destitute and oppressed and mistreated. They were too good for this world, wandering over deserts and mountains, hiding in caves and holes in the ground.

All these people earned a good reputation because of their faith, yet none of them received all that God had promised. For God had something better in mind for us, so that they would not reach perfection without us."

This passage is mostly emphasizing what a person who moves by faith can accomplish. It shows that it is neither by the might of that person nor by physical power of that person but by the faith that they have in God accomplishing what He said He would. These are regular people, people who accepted to be persecuted because of their faith. Their fight is the fact that they stood firm on their belief and did not change their posture under pressure.

The following sections will briefly present some key Biblical characters that truly exemplified the walk and fight of faith.

Abraham Moved by Faith in God

- Abraham was called out by God, out of his comfortable environment away from his parents and relatives to go to an unknown place God did not reveal, and Abraham obeyed.
- God started a covenant with him, based on that initial faith that would be the basis of salvation for those who choose to have faith in God, this can be summarized in the following verses of Genesis 12:
    - Verse 2: "I will make you into a great nation"
    - Verse 2: "I will bless you"
    - Verse 2: "I will make your name great"
    - Verse 3: "I will bless those who bless you, curse those who curse you"

    Verse 7: "I will give you this land for your offspring". The land of Canaan also known today as Palestine is given to Abraham's descendants.

God shows that His covenant was not based on Abraham's momentary failures: Abraham lied twice to avoid being killed because of his wife's beauty. He lied by saying that Sarah was not his wife, he withheld the truth that Sarah was his wife and only said that she was his sister which by the way was true.

- Once God has declared his covenant, there was an invisible fight against his faith:
    - His wife was barren and so asked Abraham to have a baby with her servant so that the covenant will be fulfilled and Abraham did, but this was not God's will
    - This led to the birth of Ishmael which represents man way of trying to achieve God's purpose through reasoning alone and not faith, so trying to do God's will by self effort and reason alone will only brings nemesis in life.
- God promised son Isaac was conceived as God declared it and was born beside all the mistakes Abraham and his wife made.
- God gave Abraham a final test: God called Abraham to sacrifice his "son, [his] only son, Isaac whom [he] loves". Abraham did not question God and was following through with the strange command of God, moving by faith in Him.

Abraham passed this great test of faith in God. Even though Abraham had his moments of failures, he always carried out what God instructed him to do. His fight of faith represents his steady belief and actions that remain consistent with what God has told him even though circumstances say otherwise.

We learn that the work of faith helps us know God in various dimensions, if we do not move by faith we will not see some dimension of God in our lives that He wants to show us.

Moses Moved by Faith in God
- First born a Hebrew in a dangerous time and sent in the wilderness as a baby to escape slaughtering decreed by Pharaoh.
- Mysteriously taken - this really means God prepared a place of training for the future mission for him - into the palace of Pharaoh and rose up as a prince of Egypt.
- Then seeking to protect his people by his own hands Moses become a murderer and fugitive, so he fled into the wilderness.
- God met him in the wilderness and got his attention with a mysterious burning bush, calling him into ministry.
- Moses initially hesitated because he was looking at his own outside appearance and ability not what God has put in him.
- Later this shy man became bold because of the presence of God with him
- Moses led millions of people out of captivity based on a direct communication with God and faith in God.
- In the wilderness, Moses' faith level was tested many times by the murmuring and complaint of the people he was leading out of Egypt but he always trusted God.
- For forty years Moses worked by faith in God for provision in the arid desert since no one else had the same type of relationship Moses had with God, all Israel lived on Moses' faith in God.

Faith is built progressively though tests of various kinds necessary for the Lord, the Author and Finisher of our faith, to build our faith. Moses faith was build gradually to meet God's plan, then from that time on God used him to carry out a very important mission for the Jewish nation and for us Christians.

We notice that Moses was endowed by an initial level of faith in Him even though he was raised as a prince, because he was bold enough to kill an Egyptian who was mistreating a slave in his presence. Wanting to be a deliverer by His own hand forced him to flee before the wrath of Pharaoh.

We learn from this that God must be the one leading us and doing the deliverance not our own will and strength. Circumstances of life will teach us and train us if we are willing to be transformed By God to His image:

Knowing this, that the trying of your faith worketh patience. But let patience have her perfect work, that ye may be perfect and entire, wanting nothing. If any of you lack wisdom, let him ask of God, that giveth to all men liberally, and upbraideth not; and it shall be given him. But let him ask in faith, nothing wavering. For he that wavereth is like a wave of the sea driven with the wind and tossed. For let not that man think that he shall receive any thing of the Lord. A double minded man is unstable in all his ways. James 1:3-10

There is a process that God is working in us and it is outside of how we think or plan our lives. This was true for Moses also who went from being prince of Egypt to being a humble shepherd for forty years in the desert with the nomadic Medianites. This also suggests that walking by faith is a little like living the life of the Medianites – nomads - who do not have a fix place to live but move from place to place in the desert according to where nature and seasons take them. Moses had to learn to surrender totally to God like nomads, delivering him from Egypt comfortable lifestyle and mindset.

Moses submitted himself to his fate and accepted it by marrying a nomad woman, having a son and settling into the nomadic life style which is sure sign of deliverance of Egypt out of him.

For our learning, it appears we also need to be comfortable in trusting God and settled in our faith in His ability to lead us in our own life before God can truly use us.

Only at that point did God start to unfold His vision to Moses to carry on His work of deliverance of his children out of Egypt.

Even at that point Moses still had to deal with some stinky thinking that he was not worthy probably because of his education from Egypt where he has seen eloquent people.

After Moses accepted the assignment he has to convince his people that God has called him to do the job.

From that time on Moses was moving by faith and solving huge problems through God using Him and he having faith that God would do what He said He would do.

Jesus Christ never did anything on his own initiative, only what He was seeing His Father doing

An excellent example of walking by faith is the following passage of Scripture:

Then said Jesus unto them, When ye have lifted up the Son of man, then shall ye know that I am he, and that I do nothing of myself; but as my Father hath taught me, I speak these things. John 8:28

This shows that Jesus was always walking by faith in the Father; He was enacting whatever the Father tells Him or what the Father was doing. Therefore God gives us all the ability to see Him in spirit so that we can move by faith but for some reason some of us have been blinded by the enemy. The good fight of faith is when we cannot see God from our natural eyes but trust Him to do all that He said in His Word He is doing.

Also, John 5:19

"Jesus gave them this answer: "I tell you the truth, the Son can do nothing by himself; he can do only what he sees his Father doing, because whatever the Father does the Son also does"

This is a strategy that would ensure us victory during our fight of faith. We should constantly be communing with Jesus (God with us) and doing what we see Him doing with our spiritual eyes.

Interlude of Jesus' Fight of Faith: Gethsemane

Then cometh Jesus with them unto a place called Gethsemane, and saith unto the disciples, Sit ye here, while I go and pray yonder. And he took with him Peter and the two sons of Zebedee, and began to be sorrowful and very heavy. Then saith he unto them, My soul is exceeding sorrowful, even unto death: tarry ye here, and watch with me. And he went a little farther, and fell on his face, and prayed, saying, O my Father, if it be possible, let this cup pass from me: nevertheless not as I will, but as thou wilt. And he cometh unto the disciples, and findeth them asleep, and saith unto Peter, What, could ye not watch with me one hour? Watch and pray, that ye enter not into temptation: the spirit indeed is willing, but the flesh is weak. He went away again the second time, and prayed, saying, O my Father, if this cup may not pass away from me, except I drink it, thy will be done. And he came and found them asleep again: for their eyes were heavy. And he left them, and went away again, and prayed the third time, saying the same words. Then cometh he to his disciples, and saith unto them, Sleep on now, and take your rest: behold, the hour is at hand, and the Son of man is betrayed into the hands of sinners. Rise, let us be going: behold, he is at hand that doth betray me. Matthew 26:36-46

This is the time when Jesus was overwhelmed by emotions of the gravity and difficulty of His assignment before it happened since He knew what was coming. His human nature was showing up and trying to distract the plan of God by trying to convince Him to give up or abort His important mission to set us free. But Jesus' unfailing faith in God the Father helped Him overcome this great temptation.

This teaches us that for us to be victorious in our assignment and life we must overcome our flesh desires that conflict with God's plan for our lives.

Jesus' Final Fight of Faith: The Cross at Golgotha

A person without spiritual understanding would say, why does He have to accept to die, it seem as though His life was wasted but the reason Jesus accepted to die is not to save his life on earth but to carry on exactly the plan of God at the right time and the right place so that redemption will be available for us all who believe in Him. He knew that letting people crucify Him was all in the plan of God and had faith in God for what He has declared long before Jesus was even born.

Faith in God will take us in directions that people would say we are out of our mind but as of the one who is hearing and obeying God he knows exactly what he or she is doing because he or she is walking by faith in God.

What we face , an unbelieving people even in the church

But know this, that in the last days perilous times will come: For men will be lovers of themselves, lovers of money, boasters, proud, blasphemers, disobedient to parents, unthankful, unholy, unloving, unforgiving, slanderers, without self-control, brutal, despisers of good, traitors, headstrong, haughty, lovers of pleasure rather than lovers of God, having a form of godliness but denying its power. And from such people turn away! For of this sort are those who creep into households and make captives of gullible women loaded down with sins, led away by various lusts, always learning and never able to come to the knowledge of the truth. Now as Jannes and Jambres resisted Moses, so do these also resist the truth: men of corrupt minds, disapproved concerning the faith; but they will progress no further, for their folly will be manifest to all, as theirs also was. 2 Timothy 3:1-9

<u>Strategy for restoration</u>

But you have carefully followed my doctrine, manner of life, purpose, faith, longsuffering, love, perseverance, persecutions, afflictions, which happened to me at Antioch, at Iconium, at Lystra—what persecutions I endured. And out of them all the Lord delivered me. Yes, and all who desire to live godly in Christ Jesus will suffer persecution. But evil men and impostors will grow worse and worse, deceiving and being deceived. But you must continue in the things which you have learned and been assured of, knowing from whom you have learned them, and that from childhood you have known the Holy Scriptures, which are able to make you wise for salvation through faith which is in Christ Jesus.

All Scripture is given by inspiration of God, and is profitable for doctrine, for reproof, for correction, for instruction in righteousness, 2 Timothy 3:10-16

Christianity requires us to lean against the wind of societal trends

Christianity is not an ideology; it is a lifestyle that honors God the Creator.

Biblical examples:

Abraham – God asked him to depart from the evil place into an unknown land away from his family, country and familiar people.

Daniel, Shadrach, Meshach and Abednego: resist and submit not to the god of the world, they kept their faith in God and were unmovable in an environment of ungodliness.

Just in case anyone is wondering about how we know we are a believer and remain in faith, the following passage of Scripture simplifies it for us:

***In fact, this is love for God: to keep his commands. And his commands are not burdensome**, 1 John 5:3*

By simply making an effort to know God's commands and keeping them we are showing that we love God which is the first and greatest commandment. Because we cannot love anyone else in the biblical sense of love if we do not love God first. His commandment includes how we are to treat other people, how to love other people, therefore by the way we treat other people we can know for ourselves if we really love God.

Every believer who truly believes is in the hall of faith of Hebrews 11. It is a terrible thing for a believer to not believe some of what God provided for his or her deliverance and abundant life. Unbelief is lethal and caused many Israelites to be severely judged by God. I pray to God in the Name of Jesus that the reader who seems to be sleeping wakes up and become aware of the importance of walking by faith and even fighting for it.

If a believer does not believe what Christ taught us then that believer is deceiving himself.

Chapter Eight: Fighting The Good Fight of Faith

"And without faith it is impossible to please God, because anyone who comes to him must believe that he exists and that he rewards those who earnestly seek him." Hebrews 11:6

Jesus said in Mark 9: 33,34 *"said unto them, 'Unto you is given the mystery of the kingdom of God: but unto them that are without, all things are done in parables: that seeing they may see, and not perceive; and hearing they hear, and not understand.'"*

But thou, O man of God, flee these things; and follow after righteousness, godliness, faith, love, patience, meekness. Fight the good fight of faith, lay hold on eternal life, whereunto thou art also called, and hast professed a good profession before many witnesses. 1 Timothy 6:11-13

But thou, O man of God, flee these things; and follow after righteousness, godliness, faith, love, patience, meekness. Fight the good fight of faith, lay hold on eternal life, whereunto thou art also called, and hast professed a good profession before many witnesses

Jesus Our Lord and Savior has already won the war and as long as we are in Him we have victory.

The good fight of faith cannot be fought with human strength. We need supernatural power to fight and be victorious. That supernatural power can only come from the source of true power that is God through the Holy Spirit. Because all have sinned and have come short before God, Jesus was sent to settle all spiritual requirements and transactions. The basis of our victory is a divine exchange. An exchange made by the Lord Jesus Christ, His natural life for our eternal salvation.

Divine exchange made by Jesus of our behalf

An excellent treatment of this transaction is done by Dereck Prince in his book: *"Blessing or Curse you can choose"*.

When we stand in a spiritual war we must stand with understanding of the basis of our victory. We are not fighting by our own might or strength or understanding or wisdom but solely on what Jesus has already completed. What Jesus has done for our salvation is already sealed and done once for all lifetimes. Jesus went through some specific punishments to acquire our total redemption.

A summary of the divine exchange made by Jesus on our behalf is the following:
1. *"The evil come upon Jesus that the corresponding good might be offered to us"* (revealed in Isaiah 53:4-5) Jesus exchanged His divine goodness with the evil that was justly destined to us.
2. *"Jesus was punished that we might be forgiven. Jesus was wounded that we might be healed"* (revealed in Isaiah 53:5-6) Jesus received the punishment that we were justly destined to us.
3. *"Jesus was made sin with our sinfulness that we might become righteous with His righteousness."* (revealed in 2 Cor. 5:21 and Isaiah 53:10) Jesus took our sins that we may become righteous in Him.
4. *"Jesus died our death that we might share His life"* (revealed in Romans 6:23) Jesus died in our place so that we do not have to die spiritually.
5. *"Jesus became poor with our poverty that we might become rich with His riches"* (revealed in Acts 20:35) Jesus took our spiritual poverty so that we can receive His spiritual riches.
6. *"Jesus bore our shame that we might share His glory. Jesus enuded our rejection that we might have His acceptance as children of God."* (revealed Ephesians 1:5-6) Jesus took our shame so that we can have access to His glory; he endured rejection that we might be adopted as children of God.
7. *"Jesus became a curse that we might receive a blessing"* (revealed in Galatians 3:13-14) Jesus even took the curses that were supposed to be for us and replaced them with a blessing.

It is therefore dangerous to boast of anything that we may have accomplished, since we can never pay our own debt before God. The exchange was shadowed in the Old Testament with the Tabernacles experience. Salvation may be free for us but it was very costly for God.

In the Tabernacles experience God set a clear pattern for His people Israel to approach Him. God instructed Moses to build a Tabernacle in the wilderness to teach His people through symbolisms revealing the redemptive plan of God for all people through the future entrance of Jesus in the Earth realm. Some of those symbols are:

- A bloody sacrifice was required at the only entrance of the court of the Tabernacle. This shows that the sinner can only be redeemed through the shedding of blood which Jesus fulfilled on the Cross for all believers. The wilderness sacrifices of animals for sins were to be done repetitively, but the sacrifice of Jesus was once for all.
- The brazen altar representing washing of the Word of God
- The Holy place where we praise God, have fellowship with each other and receive divine revelation and illumination from the Word of God.
- The Holy of Holies where the presence of God is and where the glory of God is the only source of light.

Understanding the deeper meaning of salvation

Let's go back to Abraham, the father of faith and learn about how God saved him by faith:

The LORD had said to Abram, "Leave your country, your people and your father's household and go to the land I will show you.

"I will make you into a great nation

and I will bless you;

I will make your name great,

and you will be a blessing.

I will bless those who bless you,

and whoever curses you I will curse;

and all peoples on earth

will be blessed through you."

So Abram left, as the LORD had told him; and Lot went with him. Abram was seventy-five years old when he set out from Haran. He took his wife Sarai, his nephew Lot, all the possessions they had accumulated and the people they had acquired in Haran, and they set out for the land of Canaan, and they arrived there. Abram traveled through the land as far as the site of the great tree of Moreh at Shechem. At that time the Canaanites were in the land. Genesis 12:1-6

We are going to spend more time on the first verse which I believe is the condition for a born again believer to truly walk by faith in order to receive the promised abundant life described in the remaining verses above. God said to Abraham (His name was Abram at that time):

Leave your country, your people and your father's household and go to the land I will show you.

Abraham has to:
- **Leave his country**: Abraham's original country was "Ur of the Chaldees" or "Ur Kasdim". According to Wikipedia Online, *"The traditional site of Abraham's birth is in the vicinity of Edessa — both Islamic tradition, and classical Jewish authorities such as Maimonides and Josephus, had placed Ur Kaśdim at various northern Mesopotamian sites such as Urkesh, Urartu, Urfa, or Kutha. However, in 1927 Leonard Woolley identified Ur Kaśdim with the Sumerian city of Ur, in southern Mesopotamia, which was under the rule of the Chaldeans; and this identification remains popular today"*
- **Leave his people**: the people of Ur were idolaters and false God worshippers: according to Wikipedia Online: *"The city's patron deity was Nanna, the Sumerian moon god, and the name of the city is in origin derived from the god's name, URIM2KI being the classical Sumerian spelling of LAK-32.UNUGKI, literally "the abode (UNUG) of Nanna (LAK-32)"*. So Abraham came from a background of idolatrous family environment. But it pleased God to separate Him from his people by faith.
- **And his father's household**: the relationship between the father and his children is marked by a strong soul tie. We know that Abraham father was an idol worshipper therefore that strong soul tie has powerful influence on Abraham.
- **And go** to an unspecified place.

This is the model of faith I believe God is calling us all to follow when He call us to salvation in Jesus Christ. So when we are saved we must (1) leave "our country", (2) leave "our people", (3) leave our "father's household" and (4) go to follow Jesus that we do not see.

Why do we have to leave our country when God calls us to salvation?

The understanding is not that we have to physically leave our native country but that we have to first identify ourselves as people of God before where we come from. Each country is ruled by natural as well as physical authorities who have established soul ties with all who live in the land. Because most people come from a non Christian background, they need to break from those ties to be able to be fully free to walk in faith in God.

Why do we have to leave our people when God calls us to salvation?

Again we are not necessarily talking about physically leaving our people but the Bible commands us to come out of their evil practices if we want to really walk by faith in God. If we do not break that tie, we will be seriously hindered in our walk of faith in God. For example if we know that an established tradition is not rooted in God and we are blindly following it them we can be deceived and the enemy can use it as a stronghold in our lives.

Why do we have to leave our father's household when God calls us to salvation?

We have to leave our father's house because God wants to give us a new vision of where he wants us to go. Usually the parents have their vision of the child's life that does not necessarily align with God's plan for the child; particularly when the parents are idol worshippers and witches. Also the parental tie is very strong and if the parents are ungodly they will have strong generation bondage for the children to break. Therefore when we are saved we must break from ungodly parental ties.

This is also true for a church and its members. When believers in a church become mature they must be released into their ministries that God has called them to carry on. Sometimes it may involve physically leaving the church to create another or a ministry particularly when the local church is not known to let people go. Any attempt to control individual destinies will lead to the purpose of God in the lives of those individuals being delayed or aborted.

We have faith in God and fight for our faith because what God has done and continues to do from Genesis to Revelation is clearly revealed and represents solid basis for our hope and love in Him.

In the next chapter we will present what we need to know and do to be victorious in our fight of faith.

Winning the good fight of faith

In any war, soldiers know the country or the kingdom they are fighting against. But most importantly a company of soldiers must know their immediate opponents, those they have to directly and closely fight against. In our spiritual war we must do the same, we know that Satan is the enemy but we must fight our individual fights against his foes in our territory. Our personal fights look like problems of life that we face on a daily basis.

I believe that the most powerful enemy that we have to fight against is our own evil nature, i.e. our own selves. How then can we defeat an enemy that is right in our own being with all the accesses to our lives, thoughts, finances and anything we can imagine that constitutes our privacy? Let's look more deeply at what that enemy look like.

Our triune nature

Now may the God of peace Himself sanctify you completely; and may your whole spirit, soul, and body be preserved blameless at the coming of our Lord Jesus Christ. 1 Thessalonians 5:23

A person has three parts in his being:
- the spirit,
- the soul which contains the characteristics of our personality, what makes us unique,
- and the body: which is a vessel, to contain our soul and either our old nature or God through our born again nature.

When we are saved we receive a new spirit, but we still have our soul and body. Our new born again spirit is connected to the Holy Spirit as we reconcile to God, Jesus is now our new Lord and not the devil. However the old spirit the evil nature that belongs to the devil still may have some access to our body and soul if we do not grow in Christ. Since our old nature used to control our body and soul, it wants to come back to repossess them if we are not walking by the new spirit.

The battle for the control of the soul and body is what we are engaged in the good fight of faith.

We must therefore understand who we are in Christ but also who is our primary enemy so that we can properly fight the good fight of faith.

Our true enemy

For to be carnally minded is death, but to be spiritually minded is life and peace. Because the carnal mind is enmity against God; for it is not subject to the law of God, nor indeed can be. So then, those who are in the flesh cannot please God. Romans 8:6-8.

The Bible gives us many references to this enemy of ours: evil nature, flesh or old nature. The following are true about the old nature our internal enemy:
- it was our spirit before we were born again Christians
- it is a child of the devil
- it is not able to submit to God
- it is an enmity against God
- it will not enter the Kingdom of God
- its purpose is to try to control the body and the soul that was lost to Jesus.
- It is the sinner in us, our born again nature is not a sinner
- Its objective is to kill us, to destroy us and to steal from us, there is not love in it.
- Its greatest weapon is deception, replacing what is godly and genuine with what is false, specifically it replaces
    - Love with lust
    - Faith with fear, doubt and unbelief

- Hope with hopelessness or despair
- Truth with deception and lies
- Relationship with laws and legalism
- Holiness with religious hypocrisy
- Fruit of the spirit with works of the flesh
- Reasoning together with God with reasoning alone
- Life of surrender to God to self effort

When this replacement is successful in a person's life they are deceived and fall under the control of the devil, because they lose God's perspective.

Our true nature as believers in Christ

"and that you put on the new man which was created according to God, in true righteousness and holiness." Ephesians 4:24

The Bible gives us many references to this new nature of ours:
- It is the one made in the image of God
- It is a child of God that has to grow into the fullness of Christ
- It is the one who will receive the promise that God gave to the children of God
- It cannot sin
- It always loves, hopes and has faith in God
- It is the overcomer in us
- It is at war against the evil nature for the possession of man's soul and for the control of man's body, just as Ishmael (shadow of the evil nature) and Isaac (shadow of the born again nature) fought.
- Only reasons together with God (Isaiah 1:18 " *Come now, and let us reason together," Says the LORD, " Though your sins are like scarlet, They shall be as white as snow; Though they are red like crimson, They shall be as wool.*)

How to defeat our most powerful personal enemy?

There is therefore now no condemnation to those who are in Christ Jesus,[a] who do not walk according to the flesh, but according to the Spirit. For the law of the Spirit of life in Christ Jesus has made me free from the law of sin and death. For what the law could not do in that it was weak through the flesh, God did by sending His own Son in the likeness of sinful flesh, on account of sin: He condemned sin in the flesh. Romans 8:1-3

Thank God for His redemptive plan for us through Jesus Christ who came to fulfill all the requirements for our eternal debt and deliver us from evil, by making the exchange necessary for us – meaning the new nature in us – to receive power to be victorious over all the deceptive plans of the enemy.

The Bible gives us the solution, some of which are:
- to surrender to God *"There is therefore now no condemnation to them which are in Christ Jesus, who walk not after the flesh, but after the Spirit."* Romans 8:1. Therefore to defeat the old man we must die to the old self and walk by the new spirit. Also *"I say then: Walk in the Spirit, and you shall not fulfill the lust of the flesh."* Galatians 5:16.
- to resist the devil, *"Submit yourselves therefore to God. Resist the devil, and he will flee from you."* James 4:7
- to renew our mind daily with the Word of life: *"And be not conformed to this world: but be ye transformed by the renewing of your mind, that ye may prove what is that good, and acceptable, and perfect, will of God."* Romans 12:2
- to crucify our old nature, denying flesh its desires: *"And those who are Christ's have crucified the flesh with its passions and desires."* Galatians 5:24.
- to be led by the Holy Spirit
- to always walk by faith in God, the just shall live by faith.

We need to put on the whole armor of God to stand strong against the enemy.

As Jesus did in the days of temptation in the wilderness, we must know the Word of God and use it to fight the enemy when he tempts us directly. If we do not know the Word we cannot effectively fight the enemy, though we do not fight on our own strength and knowledge of Scripture but by His Spirit. We must also put on the whole armor of God:

Therefore put on the full armor of God, so that when the day of evil comes, you may be able to stand your ground, and after you have done everything, to stand. Stand firm then, with the belt of truth buckled around your waist, with the breastplate of righteousness in place, and with your feet fitted with the readiness that comes from the gospel of peace. In addition to all this, take up the shield of faith, with which you can extinguish all the flaming arrows of the evil one. Take the helmet of salvation and the sword of the Spirit, which is the word of God. And pray in the Spirit on all occasions with all kinds of prayers and requests. With this in mind, be alert and always keep on praying for all the saints. Pray also for me, that whenever I open my mouth, words may be given me so that I will fearlessly make known the mystery of the gospel, for which I am an ambassador in chains. Pray that I may declare it fearlessly, as I should.
Ephesians 6:13-20

The Helmet

We need a spiritual head covering to be able to protect our mind from the attacks of the enemy. Since no one can function without a head, we need to protect our head with the banner of our salvation. Our mind is also a vital part of our being so the helmet will protect it from the lies of the enemy.

Breastplate

Our spiritual breastplate covering our chest is the righteousness in Christ Jesus.

Our righteousness which is the Lord Jesus covers our vital organs such as lung and heart. Proverb 4:23 says to *"Keep your heart with all diligence, For out of it spring the issues of life."* The breastplate of righteousness will help us protect our heart.

The Belt

We also need to put on the belt of truth that holds us together. We must be truthful and transparent and not given to lie and deception. As the purpose of a belt is to hold the armor together, we must walk in truth to keep our integrity.

The Shield

To protect ourselves from the frontal attacks of the devil in the evil days, we need our spiritual shield which is our faith in God. The enemy knows our behavior in the flesh but when we are walking by faith he cannot predict our next move. Therefore when we walk by faith the enemy will be powerless to succeed in his attacks against us.

The Sword

To defending ourselves and engage the enemy, we need the sword of the spirit which is the Word of God.

Prayer

Keeping the communication line open at all time with the heavenly headquarter will always give us the advantage over the enemy. In a war soldiers in the field have to communicate with their head quarters to be able to get the big picture of what the enemy is doing as well as the tactics on the ground for a particular company of soldiers.

Praise

Praising God in the mist of any circumstance, it is important to enter the gate of God with praises to God as in the wilderness tabernacles where the tribe of Judah was the one God located at the gate. God inhabit in the praises of His people, therefore when we praise God we actually cause the presence of God to be drawn to the situation.

Word of Our Testimony that Give Glory to God

Declaring what God has performed without shame and restraint:

They overcame him by the blood of the Lamb and by the word of their testimony; they did not love their lives so much as to shrink from death. **Revelation 12:11**

When we share a testimony about what God has done, it not only serves to boost the faith of the other believers but most importantly it gives the glory to God causing Him to move on our behalf to stop the enemy from making it a lie. God will never share His glory with the devil.

Have a Biblical System of self evaluation

Christ is our true role model, no human being can really truly take that role. If He could not do anything without receiving from the Father we owe to do the same, keeping our eyes on Him who is the Author and Finisher of our faith in whatever we do and obeying what He is flowing back to us..

Understanding the cross-generational implications of our walk of faith?

Manifestation of negative generational effect of Abraham's sin

Abraham lied or at least conveniently hid the truth that his wife was his sister (Gen. 12:10-20; Gen. 20:1-13 and Gen. 26:1-14), though it is true that Sarah was a sister of Abraham not from the same mother. Abraham lied three times and strangely there were two separate mentions of his descendants lying:

Strange pattern number one: Isaac the promised son of Abraham lied: Genesis 26:7-10

And the men of the place asked him of his wife; and he said, She is my sister: for he feared to say, She is my wife; lest, said he, the men of the place should kill me for Rebekah; because she was fair to look upon. And it came to pass, when he had been there a long time, that Abimelech king of the Philistines looked out at a window, and saw, and, behold, Isaac was sporting with Rebekah his wife. And Abimelech called Isaac, and said, Behold, of a surety she is thy wife; and how saidst thou, She is my sister? And Isaac said unto him, Because I said, Lest I die for her. And Abimelech said, What is this thou hast done unto us? one of the people might lightly have lien with thy wife, and thou shouldest have brought guiltiness upon us.

Strange pattern number three: Jacob the son of Isaac lied: Genesis 27:19 *And Jacob said unto his father, I am Esau thy first born; I have done according as thou badest me: arise, I pray thee, sit and eat of my venison, that thy soul may bless me.*

The implication of this pattern is that father's sin can become generational. The children will be more vulnerable to the sin of the parents even for the people of faith. This would also imply that it is possible for a person who is saved to still have to deal with generation bondage because of the sin of the fathers. Abraham was God called and justified by his faith.

Manifestation of negative generational effect of David's sin

David committed adultery with Uriah's wife Bathsheba and plotted to kill him and God retained the sin:

Because David did that which was right in the eyes of the LORD, and turned not aside from any thing that he commanded him all the days of his life, save only in the matter of Uriah the Hittite. 1 Kings 15:5.

Because of these double sins we observed the following David's Biblical lineage:

Strange pattern number one: David's son was killed as the following Biblical record shows:

Howbeit, because by this deed thou hast given great occasion to the enemies of the LORD to blaspheme, the child also that is born unto thee shall surely die. And Nathan departed unto his house. And the LORD struck the child that Uriah's wife bare unto David, and it was very sick. David therefore besought God for the child; and David fasted, and went in, and lay all night upon the earth. And the elders of his house arose, and went to him, to raise him up from the earth: but he would not, neither did he eat bread with them. And it came to pass on the seventh day, that the child died. And the servants of David feared to tell him that the child was dead: for they said, Behold, while the child was yet alive, we spake unto him, and he would not hearken unto our voice: how will he then vex himself, if we tell him that the child is dead? But when David saw that his servants whispered, David perceived that the child was dead: therefore David said unto his servants, Is the child dead? And they said, He is dead.

Strange pattern number two: David's daughter was raped and his other son murdered his brother for that, as the following Biblical record shows in 2 Samuel 13.

Strange pattern number three: Solomon had thousand seven hundred wives and three hundred concubines most from other countries not from Israel. At the end of his life some of those wives led him to spiritual adultery, by bowing to their gods.

It is important to note that David repented but the consequence of sin he committed remained and entered through his generational line.

What can you do for your own journey?

We have presented the need and the importance for a born again believer in Christ to be aware of his or her spiritual reality, believe in Jesus and to fight the good fight of faith. Now it is the reader's turn to look at his or her own life and see it from God's perspective and to see the hand of God on his or her life even from the young age while in the world. Then the reader should cooperate with God and believe that God is able to take him or her to the final destination.

I believe that to God every life counts particularly when we walk by faith in Him. There was no one in the Bible that God has used to do His divine work on earth that did not walk by faith. We who profess to be born again believers in Christ must not only walk by faith in God but we must be ready to fight for it as we would fight any body or anything precious to us. It is a display of good conscience and faith toward God.

We must realize that every aspect of our lives is fully involved in a spiritual war and we must walk by faith in all areas of life and be willing to fight for it. This may be in our prayer life, our marriage, children education, workplace, entertainment, media, politics you name it. Every area of our lives is battleground and every area of life must be submitted to God's will and we must fight to hold this position. This is what the good fight of faith is about.

The good fight of faith is not just when we go to church but mostly what happen from Monday to Saturday at home, at work, sleeping, watching the news, planning etc...

Furthermore we cannot walk by faith without surrendering our life to God. Jesus is Lord but He has to be our personal Lord ruling over every area of our lives.

We are not fighting against our brothers and sisters but we are fighting a spiritual war in which ourselves or our brother and sisters have been taken captive in some area.

This is easier said than done but this is really our reasonable service.

But every believer must come to realize that being a Christian is a spiritual commitment to trust God in every situation, it is not a show of how religious or pious or how spiritual we portray for people to see and recognize us.

If we are not fighting for our faith I would even say that we are living a lie and in hypocrisy because standing on our faith in every situation of life will challenge our flesh and its desires, it will challenge carnal Christian brothers and sisters and it will challenge the world system to choose the broad way and compromise our walk of faith.

A Biblical Picture of Living by Faith: the nomadic lifestyle

Who are nomads?

According to Merriam Webster Dictionary, a nomad is defined as " a member of a people who have no fixed residence but move from place to place usually seasonally and within a well-defined territory". Why is the life of a Christian like the life of nomads? This is because we are also to live in the world and not be part of the world.

Nomads live in the wilderness

Most of the patriarch in the Bible such as Abraham were nomads. Nomads can even be found today in northern Africa in the Sahara desert. They completely rely on the nature to live. They do however know their territory very well; they know where all they can find water and food for their flocks and for themselves. Because they rely on season and the elements to lead their daily lives. They must know the time in which they are so that they can get to the right place at the right time. As Christian we must be surrendered to God the same way and let God lead us in the direction He desires.

The nomads are known to live very simple lives since they are always on the move. We Christian must have the same mentality that we are only passing through the earth and should not settle with the standard of the world system.

Nomads live for what they believe

The whole life of the nomad is involved in the belief of what their God is leading them taking from the Biblical patriarchs. They have times of worship but there every life activity is involved in their belief in God. God is at the center of their lives just as the wilderness tabernacle was at the center of the camp. We should learn from the lifestyle of the nomads.

If you were a horse back rider, how would you like your horse to be when you are trying to get on it?

Would you want the horse to stand still?

Would you want it to keep going steadily in a predictable direction and speed?

Or would you prefer it to be jumping aimlessly and widely when you are trying to get on it?

These are some interesting questions that are quite relevant to our walk with God and our faith in Him. We too are like horses that the Lord wants to use since we are vessels. The Bible says in Acts 9:15 (KJV) *"But the Lord said unto him, Go thy*

way: for he is a chosen vessel unto me, to bear my name before the Gentiles, and kings, and the children of Israel:" So for the Lord to use us we need to have a faith attitude of either:
- Moving in faith without wavering (as in "1 Corinthians 4:2 *Moreover it is required in stewards, that a man be found faithful.*") or
- Standing still waiting in faith waiting on the Lord (as in "Psalms 46:10: *Be still, and know that I am God: I will be exalted among the heathen, I will be exalted in the earth*")

The Lord wants to find us busy doing good works by faith in Him or waiting by standing still before Him.

It takes faith to defeat your Goliath?

The Bible story of the fight between David and Goliath in 1 Samuel 17 is very revealing on how to defeat the strong man-enemy in your own life. David understood this and applied this understanding to defeat Goliath. Now the defeat of Goliath itself was a faith boosting event because the Israelites who were terrified and were in hiding as Goliath the Philistine defied them and insulted them, were emboldened to rise from their hiding place and pursue and overtake the army of the enemy.

What is the key to being successful in our faith walk?

The revelation of that key is hidden inside the command of God to Abraham during the call of God on his life in Genesis 12: 1-2 "*Now the LORD had said unto Abram, Get thee out of thy country, and from thy kindred, and from thy father's house, unto a land that I will shew thee: And I will make of thee a great nation, and I will bless thee, and make thy name great; and thou shalt be a blessing:*"

When God call us there something that we have to be very diligent in letting go for good to be successful in our faith walk with God:
- Our country: we must not first be defined by where we come from but by our God. There are territorial authorities that have influence on the lives of those who originate from a particular territory.
- Our family: because there some ties that need to be cut with are parents to be able to walk by faith in God otherwise those ties will bind you and lead you to failures in your faith walk. Abraham learned this the hard way when he took Lot with him when God called him. We must first be defined by our God rather than in what family we come from.
- Our father's house: because there are strong generation bondages and soul ties that need to be broken if one is to walk by faith in God

To be victorious in our fight of faith we need to be constant visionaries like Jesus our Lord?

The faith walk and fight is easier if we can use our spiritual sense to see what the Lord is doing and telling us to do in the present. Jesus Himself never did anything in His own initiative:

Then answered Jesus and said unto them, Verily, verily, I say unto you, The Son can do nothing of himself, but what he seeth the Father do: for what things soever he doeth, these also doeth the Son likewise. John 5:19

If Jesus never acted alone and from his own initiative, and he is our Lord and model, we should also do the same in our faith walk. We should exercise our spiritual senses to be able to perceive what God is doing in our lives, the lives of the family members, in the community and in the world. Also in John 2:28 the Lord said the same thing:

Then said Jesus unto them, When ye have lifted up the Son of man, then shall ye know that I am he, and that I do nothing of myself; but as my Father hath taught me, I speak these things.

Our faith walk should involve seeing in the spiritual dimension with spiritual senses as we become mature believers in Christ Jesus.

I want to be a believer who experience the following *"He that believeth on me, as the scripture hath said, out of his belly shall flow rivers of living water."* (John 7:38). Believers should flow with the Holy Spirit in order to be victorious faith walkers.

Moving from Head-Faith to Heart-Faith

Most of us raised up in the Western education system have grown up trusting what we have learn or our intellectual ability more than our intuitions coming from our heart. This is also true for most Christians in the Western world who tend to trust their own wisdom more than what the Scripture clearly teaches. But until we move from head understanding to heart understanding we will not really move in faith. Head understanding alone only produces belief with no action while heart understanding produces belief accompanied by action. Head understanding only may also lead to religious bondage just like the Pharisees. James explains this truth in the following passage of Scripture:

What does it profit, my brethren, if someone says he has faith but does not have works? Can faith save him? If a brother or sister is naked and destitute of daily food, and one of you says to them, "Depart in peace, be warmed and filled," but you do not give them the things which are needed for the body, what does it profit? Thus also faith by itself, if it does not have works, is dead. But someone will say, "You have faith, and I have works." Show me your faith without your works, and I will show you my faith by my works. You believe that there is one God. You do well. Even the demons believe—and tremble! But do you want to know, O foolish man, that faith without works is dead? James 2:14-20

A miracle always happens when we mix our faith with *heart* believing action, if our heart does not really believe but only our head there will be no miracle. The story of Peter walking on the water teaches that important principle:

And Peter answered Him and said, "Lord, if it is You, command me to come to You on the water." So He said, "Come." And when Peter had come down out of the boat, he walked on the water to go to Jesus. But when he saw that the wind was boisterous, he was afraid; and beginning to sink he cried out, saying, "Lord, save me!" Matthew 14:28-30

We also see that when we cease from believing in our heart we cause the miracle to cease. So when we stop believing in our heart we cease to receive what God intended for us to receive in that moment. Furthermore our heart-believing is linked to our keeping God's perspective and focusing on Jesus the Author and Finisher of our faith. Anytime we lose focus of God's perspective or stop focusing on Jesus we move out of faith. The key to overcoming unbelief is to set our eyes on Jesus as the following passage of Scriptures teaches:

Therefore we also, since we are surrounded by so great a cloud of witnesses, let us lay aside every weight, and the sin which so easily ensnares us, and let us run with endurance the race that is set before us, looking unto Jesus, the author and finisher of our faith, who for the joy that was set before Him endured the cross, despising the shame, and has sat down at the right hand of the throne of God. Hebrews 12:1-3

To grow in faith we must set our spiritual eyes on Jesus who is the Author and Perfecter of our faith.

The following passages of Scripture emphasize the importance of believing in our heart:

For assuredly, I say to you, whoever says to this mountain, 'Be removed and be cast into the sea,' and does not doubt in his heart, but believes that those things he says will be done, he will have whatever he says. Mark 11:22-23

Miracles only happen when we believe in our heart what we are asking God, if we doubt in our heart we will not receive anything we asking from God as Hebrews 11:6 says it so vividly *"And without faith it is impossible to please God, because anyone who comes to him must believe that he exists and that he rewards those who earnestly seek him."* Believing in our heart and not doubting in our heart is an area where Jesus consistently rebuked His disciples:

Later He appeared to the eleven as they sat at the table; and He rebuked their unbelief and hardness of heart, because they did not believe those who had seen Him after He had risen.

Mark 16:13

Now the enemy also seems to understand the importance of a believer believing in his heart so he directs his attacks on that very area:

Those by the wayside are the ones who hear; then the devil comes and takes away the word out of their hearts, lest they should believe and be saved. Luke 8:11-12 . Also,

Above all else, guard your heart, for it is the wellspring of life. Proverbs 4:23

The enemy targets our heart to attack it because it is the wellspring of our lives.

So therefore it is not only hearing in the head but we must hear in our heart to truly believe in Jesus.

Then He said to them, "O foolish ones, and slow of heart to believe in all that the prophets have spoken! Luke 24:24-25

We can be slow to believe in our heart if we keep on having a mental acknowledgement of the Word of God but do not put what we have heard into action. James 2:20 says *"But do you want to know, O foolish man, that faith without works is dead?"*

I strongly believe that the goal of any Christian is to be able to get to the point where we believe in Christ in such a way that the Holy Spirit is freely flowing from us: *He who believes in Me, as the Scripture has said, out of his heart will flow rivers of living water."* John 7:37-38

Many times Jesus has to give command to people He was about to minister to not fear nor be afraid since fear will drive out faith, hindering the flow of the Holy Spirit. For example Jesus said in John 14:1 *"Let not your heart be troubled; you believe in God, believe also in Me.*

Many times we do not get what we pray for because we do not believe with our whole heart: *Then Philip said, "If you believe with all your heart, you may." And he answered and said, "I believe that Jesus Christ is the Son of God."* Acts 8:37

Even the salvation experience must be a spiritual experience not just mental:

that if you confess with your mouth the Lord Jesus and believe in your heart that God has raised Him from the dead, you will be saved. Romans 10:9 and *For with the heart one believes unto righteousness, and with the mouth confession is made unto salvation.* Romans 10:10

Our faith that moves God must originate from a spiritual experience:

You worship what you do not know; we know what we worship, for salvation is of the Jews. But the hour is coming, and now is, when the true worshipers will worship the Father in spirit and truth; for the Father is seeking such to worship Him. God is Spirit, and those who worship Him must worship in spirit and truth." John 4:22-24

Most of us educated in the Western education system which seeks to develop the left brain more than the right, have a heart time moving from head belief or head-faith (if there is such a thing), to heart belief or heart faith which is the only one that would move God.

Three areas of our lives where our faith must be visible and show good testimony for the glory of God

There are three areas of a human being that affect his whole lifetime: time, money and relationship.

First let's look at time.

Use of our life time:

We spend time in many activities that we consider important, but we often do not really look at the usage of our time from an eternal perspective. We are born and live for about seventy to eighty years on average and based on our daily, weekly, monthly and yearly habit and tradition we can pretty much evaluate how much time we wasted, how much time we used to do God's will and how much time we used to the enemy's will. We know that the enemy's purpose is to kill, to steal and to destroy and the purpose of our Lord Jesus in our lives is to give us life and give more abundantly. So we can pretty much evaluate how much of one's life is used for dead works and how much for good works.

The question is, at the end of my life what testimony concerning the usage of my time on earth do I leave? Did I spend most of my time in dead works or did spend my time in good works.

The eternal perspective mindset of time usage is to not waste time on things that do have positive eternal effect. One way we can do so is to set aside a time for building relationship with God, a time for family, work and relationship building. The time we use to do wasteful things can add up pretty quickly: watching TV, playing video games, etc ..., things that are destined to "kill" time are really counting negatively against us and constitute dead works if they are not used to build relationships. We can still moderately do those things if they have a purpose of edifying ourselves or others or to build good relationships.

Use of our life time money:

Questions like how much money will I earn and spend over my lifetime, how much money did contribute to the building of the Kingdom of God are not

Usually even thought of by most people. However this is another element beside time that show a testimony of our lives. Do we mostly spend our money on dead works or do we invest it in good works? Do we have a positive lifetime net worth at the end of our lives or did we leave our families in a net debt? A great testimony of our lives as Christian should show at least ten percent investment in the building of the Kingdom of God and we should not die in debt.

Lifetime relationships:

Our lifetime relationships are the third dimension of life we must come positive on, at the end of our lives. Did we diligently work to build good relationships in our lives or did we take advantage of people and isolate ourselves as we get old? Every Christian must have an eternal mindset and look at earthly life as an investment to good works to produces relationships that honor God and reconcile Him with lost people.

So looking at these three dimensions of life we can ask ourselves how am I doing? Am I purposely investing my time, my money to do good works? Am I carefully and intentionally building others up and helping them connect to the Father or am I living a selfish isolated life? Fighting the good fight of faith requires that we are optimally using the resources God endowed us with to invest in His Kingdom to produce eternal returns.

Crossroad of our faith

Every faith walker will one day stand at a turning point where he must make a bold move based on his faith in God. This is as if he was at the top of a steep mountain and something is telling him to just trust that when he lets go and jump that something he does not see will catch him. For Abraham it was obeying God's voice to get out of his own country, family and father's house to go to an unspecified land; it was also carrying out the command of God to sacrifice his God promised son Isaac. For Moses it was him being able to face Pharaoh and tell him to let his people go in the name of God. For Joshua it was to obey the command of God to simply walk around the fortified city of Jericho seven times and shout to destroy it as God commanded. For Peter it was walking on the water when he saw Jesus doing the same. That step seems quite scary because it is contrary to reason and we are generally tempted to give up because of self preservation. But this moment should be a moment of victory of heart over our mind to fully trust in God and allow the spirit to lead us. This should not be a mind originated test of our faith but a heart conviction originated test of our faith and it should normally be as a result of God's command to do it in that moment. If the mind alone decides to test it will not work.

For many of us this is a test that comes as simple as taking a stand at our workplace for God or deciding to do the godly thing even if it hurts or cost us something. There is a clear pattern when God takes us through this process. By analyzing the story of Shadrach Meshach and Abednego:

And commanded some of the strongest soldiers in his army to tie up Shadrach, Meshach and Abednego and throw them into the blazing furnace. So these men, wearing their robes, trousers, turbans and other clothes, were bound and thrown into the blazing furnace. The king's command was so urgent and the furnace so hot that the flames of the fire killed the soldiers who took up Shadrach, Meshach and Abednego, and these three men, firmly tied, fell into the blazing furnace. Then King Nebuchadnezzar leaped to his feet in amazement and asked his advisers, "Weren't there three men that we tied up and threw into the fire?" They replied, "Certainly, O king." He said, "Look! I see four men walking around in the fire, unbound and unharmed, and the fourth looks like a son of the gods." Nebuchadnezzar then approached the opening of the blazing furnace and shouted, "Shadrach, Meshach and Abednego, servants of the Most High God, come out! Come here!" So Shadrach, Meshach and Abednego came out of the fire, and the satraps, prefects, governors and royal advisers crowded around them. They saw that the fire had not harmed their bodies, nor was a hair of their heads singed; their robes were not scorched, and there was no smell of fire on them. Then Nebuchadnezzar said, "Praise be to the God of Shadrach, Meshach and Abednego, who has sent his angel and rescued his servants! They trusted in him and defied the king's command and were willing to give up their lives rather than serve or worship any god except their own God. Therefore I decree that the people of any nation or language who say anything against the God of Shadrach, Meshach and Abednego be cut into pieces and their houses be turned into piles of rubble, for no other god can save in this way." Then the king promoted Shadrach, Meshach and Abednego in the province of Babylon. Daniel 3:20-30.

We learn at least three important principles here:

First, the three Hebrew boys could have died even before they were thrown into the fire but they did not. Instead the soldiers who were throwing them in the fire died because of the heat. So if God is taking us through a test that requires a bold faith move, we know that His intention is not to kill us otherwise we would die before we even get in the test.

Second, when we move in faith and are now inside the very thing that the enemy wants to use to kill us, we are free. So the fire that we find ourselves in has a liberating power. Why do we say that? Because the Hebrew boys were bound being thrown in the fire but once there the Lord met them and loosed them and were walking in the fire unharmed. The lesson for us to learn is that we are going through something as a result of boldly moving on our faith in God, God will be with us inside the fire or the tribulation, and it is then that we are free.

Third, at the end of the move of faith God gets greater glory and we get promoted. When King Nebuchadnezzar saw the Hebrew boys come out unharmed, he praised God and acknowledged Him, then he promoted the Hebrew boys in the province of Babylon.

Now God expect from each one of us to be able to go through that test so that He can get the glory and promote us to our next level in faith, unfortunately most of us do not go through with the test and get the promised victory because of unbelief and fear. Fear being our worst enemy.

The sin of fear

Fearing anything else other than God is a sin because it is as if we believed what devil would do to us more than we believe in God. The origin of that type of fear is the devil:

There is no fear in love; but perfect love casteth out fear: because fear hath torment. He that feareth is not made perfect in love. 1 John 4:18

Because God is love, if we have God we should not fear anyone or anything else. Here are some key verses that gives us command to not fear or be afraid since that cancels our faith in that moment:

Say to him, 'Be careful, keep calm and don't be afraid. Do not lose heart because of these two smoldering stubs of firewood—because of the fierce anger of Rezin and Aram and of the son of Remaliah. Isaiah 7:4

When we fear, we lose heart meaning our heart is no longer in control, flesh takes over. We know that if we walk by flesh we will only fulfill the desires of the evil nature.

So don't be afraid; you are worth more than many sparrows. Matthew 10:31

When we fear we reduce ourselves, we lose God's perspective about ourselves we no longer believe who we are in God.

But Jesus came and touched them. "Get up," he said. "Don't be afraid." Matthew 17:7

Ignoring what they said, Jesus told the synagogue ruler, "Don't be afraid; just believe." Mark 5:36

Hearing this, Jesus said to Jairus, "Don't be afraid; just believe, and she will be healed." Luke 8:50

Jesus often gives the command to not be afraid before he heals that person.

But Jesus immediately said to them: "Take courage! It is I. Don't be afraid." Matthew 14:27

Immediately he spoke to them and said, "Take courage! It is I. Don't be afraid." Then he climbed into the boat with them, and the wind died down. They were completely amazed, Mark 6:51

Then Jesus said to Simon, "Don't be afraid; from now on you will catch men." So they pulled their boats up on shore, left everything and followed him. Luke 5:11

Jesus encourage His disciples and often tells them not to be afraid and instead to have faith.

The good fight of faith is an on-going fight

When we look at the whole process of God's deliverance of the Israelites from Egyptian bondage, we learn a few things about faith.

God promised to deliver His people Israel from Egyptian slavery and raised up Moses to carry that on. The promise of God to the forefathers was to take the people of Israel to the Promise Land on the other side of the Jordan River where flows milk and honey. The circumstances certainly did not look like that would happen in the eyes of the Israelites who have to spend forty years in the wilderness desert even though God was providing for them on a daily basis and performing miracles human being have never experienced.

The struggle of every circumstance was whether the Israelites would believe God to really do what He has already said He would do. They grumbled, rebelled against Moses and against God causing some to perish in the wilderness. But the ultimate test was when they were in the neighborhood of the land God has promised them, right on this side of the Jordan River. The story is found in Numbers 13:26-33 specifically:

Now they departed and came back to Moses and Aaron and all the congregation of the children of Israel in the Wilderness of Paran, at Kadesh; they brought back word to them and to all the congregation, and showed them the fruit of the land. Then they told him, and said: "We went to the land where you sent us. It truly flows with milk and honey, and this is its fruit. Nevertheless the people who dwell in the land are strong; the cities are fortified and very large; moreover we saw the descendants of Anak there. The Amalekites dwell in the land of the South; the Hittites, the Jebusites, and the Amorites dwell in the mountains; and the Canaanites dwell by the sea and along the banks of the Jordan." Then Caleb quieted the people before Moses, and said, "Let us go up at once and take possession, for we are well able to overcome it." But the men who had gone up with him said, "We are not able to go up against the people, for they are stronger than we." And they gave the children of Israel a bad report of the land which they had spied out, saying, "The land through which we have gone as spies is a land that devours its inhabitants, and all the people whom we saw in it are men of great stature. There we saw the giants[d] (the descendants of Anak came from the giants); and we were like grasshoppers in our own sight, and so we were in their sight."

Ten out of the twelve spies came back with bad reports, they have forgotten all the great miracles God has performed from Egypt through the wilderness every day for forty years. The look at the people in the land God promised them as too powerful for them! But Joshua and Caleb among the spies believed God's report and kept their faith in God. The sad part of the story is that God allowed those who brought the bad report as well as all those of the congregation of Israel who believed them to die in the wilderness not being able to enter the Promise Land because of their unbelief.

Then after those who have faith crossed the Jordan River to enter the Land of Promise there was another test of their faith waiting for them. God gave some seemingly strange instructions on how the fortified city of Jericho will be destroyed:

Now Jericho was securely shut up because of the children of Israel; none went out, and none came in. And the LORD said to Joshua: "See! I have given Jericho into your hand, its king, and the mighty men of valor. You shall march around the city, all you men of war; you shall go all around the city once. This you shall do six days. And seven priests shall bear seven trumpets of rams' horns before the ark. But the seventh day you shall march around the city seven times, and the priests shall blow the trumpets. It shall come to pass, when they make a long blast with the ram's horn, and when you hear the sound of the trumpet, that all the people shall shout with a great shout; then the wall of the city will fall down flat. And the people shall go up every man straight before him." Then Joshua the son of Nun called the priests and said to them, "Take up the ark of the covenant, and let seven priests bear seven trumpets of rams' horns before the ark of the LORD." And he said to the people, "Proceed, and march around the city, and let him who is armed advance before the ark of the LORD." Joshua 6:1-7

Again the faith of some people in the congregation of Israel started to fail because the story seem to strange to believe when Joshua related the instructions of God to them.

But it happens just the way God said it would:

So the people shouted when the priests blew the trumpets. And it happened when the people heard the sound of the trumpet, and the people shouted with a great shout, that the wall fell down flat. Then the people went up into the city, every man straight before him, and they took the city. And they utterly destroyed all that was in the city, both man and woman, young and old, ox and sheep and donkey, with the edge of the sword. Joshua 6:20-21

The one thing that we can consistently see is that God has never failed to carry out what He said He would carry out, He always fulfill His part of the bargain faithfully. We must meet Him faithfully by faith to be victorious.

The story of faith goes on for the people of Israel till this day. From Joshua to David to Jehoshaphat to the president of the present day Israel, the people of God have to move by faith at every circumstance of life. We can even see today how the land of Israel is besieged by hostile countries around them but God delivered them every day and continue to do so in the future as long as the Israelites continue to put their faith in God.

We Christians, saved by faith in Jesus Christ, descendant of Abraham and Sarah the father and mother of faith, also have the same path to follow. We must walk by faith in God at every circumstance of our life. We too will go through many trials and tribulations but we must keep our faith to be victorious.

At the very end of time, Christian believers will have no choice but to stand firm on their faith in the Lord Jesus Christ because the good fight of faith will become not only spiritual but physical as well.

It is not by might nor by power

It is however important to emphasize that the choice to live optimally heavenly minded cannot be fully accomplished without the input from our inner man. Galatians 2:20 says

I have been crucified with Christ and I no longer live, but Christ lives in me. The life I now live in the body, I live by faith in the Son of God, who loved me and gave himself for me.

So I- meaning the old man - is dead or should be dead and the new man, meaning the Christ in us should be fully alive in us and leading our lives for the optimal Christian life that optimizes time and money to be possible.

It is not the will power that can focus a person to have the heavenly perspective while making every decision; this has to be born of the Spirit. John 3:6 says *That which is born of the flesh is flesh; and that which is born of the Spirit is spirit.* So discipline without heart conviction will not produce a life that optimizes every life moment for an eternal perspective.

How did Jesus spend His time on Earth?

Because the Lord Jesus is our example of Christian life, we cannot end without looking at the standard He has left us to follow.

Jesus spent significant time in Prayer

Jesus spent a lot of time with the Father in solitude and in prayers. The following passages of Scripture testify of this fact:

And when he had sent the multitudes away, he went up into a mountain apart to pray: and when the evening was come, he was there alone. Matthew 14:23

And in the morning, rising up a great while before day, he went out, and departed into a solitary place, and there prayed. Mark 1:35

And it came to pass in those days, that he went out into a mountain to pray, and continued all night in prayer to God. Luke 6:12

And it came to pass, as he was alone praying, his disciples were with him: and he asked them, saying, Whom say the people that I am? Luke 9:18

And it came to pass, that, as he was praying in a certain place, when he ceased, one of his disciples said unto him, Lord, teach us to pray, as John also taught his disciples. Luke 11:1

It is clear that Jesus spent a lot of time praying to the Father. The lesson for us is to be able to allocate quality time with God, the true source of power, authority, strength knowledge etc …

Jesus spent time helping people

One other activity that Jesus spent a lot of time in was ministering to people.

Numerous passages of Scripture describe Jesus healing the sick casting out demons, speaking the good news of the Kingdom of God to the lost, feeding the hungry etc …

The lesson of our faith walk is to take significant time to help others.

Jesus spent time teaching his disciples

Another activity that Jesus spent a lot of time in was teaching His disciples the Word of God, implementing before them what He was teaching, using life examples to teach them. The disciples were later to do what He was doing and even more.

We learn here that we need to reproduce ourselves unto good works so that those coming after us will do the same for the glory of God.

This chapter was all about showing the reality of the walk of faith through lifetime balance sheets in time and money in such a way that the reader will become aware of the importance of the choices we make on the daily basis. Those choices add up to show a true life testimony of our faith in God for we must show our faith with our work. No longer should we only be mental Christians but heart Christians for God is seeking those who would worship Him in spirit and in truth not in cliché or in religious perfection. I should hope that the reader has become more aware of their reality of faith and the need to even fight to death for it. May the Lord open and enlighten the eye of our understanding, that we may know what the hope of His calling is, and that Christ may richly dwell in our heart by faith, "*being rooted and grounded in love*".

The perfect example of faith walking is the life of Jesus our Lord and role model. So then for us to walk by faith we must be totally dependent on God just as Jesus never did anything on His own or out of His own initiative, we must be fully surrendered to God with all that He has put in us. Jesus obeyed the Father even to the death. So we as Christians must renew our mind and accept the fact that "*I have been crucified with Christ; it is no longer I who live, but Christ lives in me; and the life which I now live in the flesh I live by faith in the Son of God, who loved me and gave Himself for me.*" Therefore I do not do what I want but do what Jesus my Lord wants.

Hebrews 11:6 is clearly declaring the basic requirement for the life of the Christian:

And without faith it is impossible to please God, because anyone who comes to him must believe that he exists and that he rewards those who earnestly seek him.

Therefore for the Christian, faith is not optional because we would be deceiving ourselves if we say we put God first but do not use our money and time – or our treasure – to honor Him first. For where our heart is there will our treasure be also. And that is the ultimate test.

Lord I pray that you deliver me from unbelief and help me to walk by faith in all areas of my life, that I will have heart faith in the Lord and in His Word. I also pray that every single person who will read this dissertation will overcome his or her unbelief and truly believe from his or her heart what the Word of God says and act accordingly in Jesus Name, Amen.

Looking at the Bible from a different perspective

Let's say that you do not know how to swim and you find yourself in the middle of the Ocean holding on to a piece of log. You look around and you see sharks all over and people being devoured by the sharks alive, some already dead and you see a good Samaritan from an helicopter throwing a rope for you to grab so that you can get out of that environment. Let me ask you this question, if you were that person in that environment will you hold on to the rope with all your strength or will you try to analyze it and waste your time asking yourself if this is a real rope or a fake one? I believe the Bible is the same way to everyone living on the earth. It is something to solidly grab to and not let go, it is something that our whole life depends on, something that we do not waste our time trying to build doctrines on but something to receive and live by to the best of our understanding and because God gives us the Holy Spirit, He will lead us into all truth. When we get it wrong He will help us correct it. The Bible says

For everyone who asks receives; the one who seeks finds; and to the one who knocks, the door will be opened. "Which of you, if your son asks for bread, will give him a stone? Or if he asks for a fish, will give him a snake? If you, then, though you are evil, know how to give good gifts to your children, how much more will your Father in heaven give good gifts to those who ask him! So in everything, do to others what you would have them do to you, for this sums up the Law and the Prophets. Matthew 7:8-12

God is not a liar, if we are seeking Him, because He is in control of all things including the spiritual world, He is able to lead us into all truth so that we will not err in our search, the enemy cannot succeed in deceiving us if we seek God with our whole heart in faith.

Conclusion

In conclusion we must recognize that the life of Abraham itself is an example of how to be victorious in our faith walk with God. Abraham made some mistakes but overall He was faithful to the call of God. Therefore God is not looking for supermen but for ordinary people who would trust Him enough to follow Him as

Abraham did. Walking by faith is something we grow into and may not happen overnight. We all receive a measure of faith as a seed that we must take care of so that it can reach maturity.

Faith involves a plain explanation of things that science cannot explain, a believer is one that should receive fully the divine explanation without questions. If any questions exist then the person is not truly a believer of the divine doctrine. For one to be a believer one must take the full doctrine as face value even those sub-doctrine that go against reason. There should not be any input of the believer to the divine doctrine, the whole divine doctrine must be taken and believed or completely rejected. Thank God it is not a decision that the flesh can make but only the one who the Spirit of God leads to do so and to pursue, therefore it is not out of reach but we must be willing, we must be believe and be diligent in our seeking the Lord. We must seek God with our whole heart. WHOLE HEART is the key. Let's continue pondering on the following passages:

I will praise You, O LORD, with my whole heart; I will tell of all Your marvelous works.Psalm 9:1

Praise the LORD!I will praise the LORD with my whole heart, In the assembly of the upright and in the congregation. Psalm 111:1

Blessed are those who keep His testimonies, Who seek Him with the whole heart! Psalm 119:2

With my whole heart I have sought You; Oh, let me not wander from Your commandments! Psalm 119:10

Give me understanding, and I shall keep Your law; Indeed, I shall observe it with my whole heart. Psalm 119:34

I entreated Your favor with my whole heart; Be merciful to me according to Your word. Psalm 119:58

The proud have forged a lie against me, But I will keep Your precepts with my whole heart. Psalm 119:69

I cry out with my whole heart; Hear me, O LORD! I will keep Your statutes.

Psalm 119:145

I will praise You with my whole heart; Before the gods I will sing praises to You. Psalm 138:1

Why should you be stricken again? You will revolt more and more. The whole head is sick, And the whole heart faints. Isaiah 1:5

And yet for all this her treacherous sister Judah has not turned to Me with her whole heart, but in pretense," says the LORD. Jeremiah 3:10

Then I will give them a heart to know Me, that I am the LORD; and they shall be My people, and I will be their God, for they shall return to Me with their whole heart. Jeremiah 24:7

May the Lord give us understand of this meditation and enlightens our heart to grasp the full impact of this message that you may fight the good fight of faith in Jesus Christ.

www.ingramcontent.com/pod-product-compliance
Lightning Source LLC
Chambersburg PA
CBHW081500040426
42446CB00016B/3322